Researching Sing Up's Workforce Development

main findings from the first three years

practitioners' singing self-efficacy and knowledge about singing

London: imerc

Researching Sing Up's Workforce Development
main findings from the first three years
practitioners' singing self-efficacy and knowledge about singing

Evangelos Himonides
Jo Saunders
Ioulia Papageorgi
Graham Welch

ISBN13: 978-1-905351-14-5
ISBN10: 1-905351-14-3

Copyright © 2011 Evangelos Himonides & Graham Welch

Published in Great Britain in 2011
International Music Education Research Centre (imerc)
http://www.imerc.org
Department of Arts and Humanities
Institute of Education
University of London
20, Bedford Way
London WC1H 0AL
United Kingdom

Copy requests:
Dr Evangelos Himonides
e.himonides@ioe.ac.uk

Typeset in Frutiger

British Library Cataloguing-in-Publication Data
A CIP record is available from the British Library

All rights reserved. Except for the quotation of short passages for the purposes of criticism or review, no part of this publication may be reproduced, stored in a retrieval system, or transmitted, in any form or by any means, electronic, mechanical, photocopying, recording or otherwise, without prior permission from the publisher.

Executive summary

- Over one thousand respondents participated in the Sing Up workforce development research evaluation surveys.
- The majority of respondents were female, a proportion that is in line with published school staffing statistics, as well as survey response trends.
- There was a representative distribution of responses across all respondent age-groups.
- Although all local authorities in England were represented, 50% of respondents were from 15% of those possible.
- Approximately one in two respondents held a qualification in singing and/or music.
- Almost 70% of the respondents' had Qualified Teacher Status (QTS).
- Almost three in four respondents reported not being interested additionally in pursuing a Masters in Teaching & Learning (a new government-funded practice-based masters programme) as part of their professional development planning.
- Although the majority of respondents taught/lead children aged 7+ to 10+ years (Key Stage 2 pupils), all Primary school ages and year groups were represented in the survey data.
- One in three participants did not have a formal responsibility for music in their schools.
- In one component of the survey, participants were invited to respond to 72 statements. These were organised in six thematic groups that covered aspects of their own singing skills and their ability to lead singing development in children.

- The data captured by the online survey instrument demonstrated an extremely high internal statistical consistency in terms of respondents' answers.
- The data analyses suggest that the Sing Up workforce development experience was perceived as positive and increased in accordance with the number of sessions attended.

Detailed analyses of responses to both sets of closed and open questions revealed that the Sing Up professional development had led to very positive impacts on their children's singing.

- Two main benefits were reported by respondents: an increase of their self confidence as vocal leaders and an appreciation of the provision of teaching materials to support the teaching of singing in schools. They were also positive about having access to a peer support network amongst fellow professionals.
- Respondents also reported that their professional development experiences confirmed a view that 'all children can be successful' in singing.
- Singing was seen to help cultivate a heightened sense of community and to impact positively on children's social and emotional development.
- Teachers reported that their Sing Up experience had provided detailed guidance about singing and also vocal health.
- The vast majority of respondents stated that they had taken the opportunity back in the workplace to share their Sing Up development experiences with colleagues.

Contents

Executive summary	1
Contents	5
List of figures	8
List of tables	9
Introduction	10
Respondents' demographic data	12
Research strands	12
Respondents' sex	12
Respondents' age-groups	13
Respondents' qualifications in Music and/or Singing	17
Qualified teacher's status	18
Masters in Teaching & Learning	19
Pupil (student) age groups being lead or taught	20
Formal responsibility for music in participants' schools	21
Local authority	23
Internal consistency of the survey	25
Participants' singing self-efficacy	26
Knowledge of learners	30
Knowledge of Singing Pedagogy	35
Knowledge of Musics	39
The pupils is my group/class	43
My teaching/singing leadership	47
Qualitative data analyses	51
What changes have you seen in the children that you work with since receiving your Sing Up training?	51
Overview	*51*
Detail	*52*
What changes in your own practice have you noticed since receiving training?	54
Overview	*54*
Detail	*54*

Please offer some information regarding your own or your pupils' emotional experiences during singing? 56

Overview *56*
Detail *56*

Is singing important to you and the children that you work with? 58

Overview *58*
Detail *58*

If you are a teacher, have you ever had any training in vocal health? 60

Overview *60*
Detail *61*

Have you suffered illness and time from work due to poor vocal health or loss of voice? 62

Overview *62*
Detail *62*

Have you shared anything that you have learned in this Sing Up training scheme with your colleagues? 63

Overview *63*
Detail *64*

What commitment have you made to continue developing your own singing and the singing of children? 66

Overview *66*
Detail *66*

Further comments 69

Overview *69*
Detail *69*

Conclusion 72

Appendix I: List of reported qualifications in Music and/or Singing 73

Appendix II: Respondents' qualifications in music and/or singing across the research strands 84

Appendix III: QTS (strands) 86

Appendix IV: Masters in Teaching & Learning (other) 88

Appendix V: Groups normally lead 89

Appendix VI: 'Other' formal responsibilities for music in school 92

Appendix VII: Local authorities 98

Appendix VIII: Local Authority representation across research strands 103

Appendix IX: Self efficacy, sex 105

Appendix X: Self efficacy, QTS 106

Appendix XI: Self efficacy, number of Sing Up training activities 107

Appendix XII: Knowledge of learners, sex 109

Appendix XIII: Knowledge of learners, QTS 110

Appendix XIV: Knowledge of learners, number of Sing Up training activities	111
Appendix XV: ANOVA - Knowledge of learners, number of Sing Up training activities	113
One-way Analysis of Variance (ANOVA)	113
Post Hoc Tests	113
Appendix XVI: Knowledge of singing pedagogy, sex	115
Appendix XVII: Knowledge of singing pedagogy, QTS	116
Appendix XVIII: Knowledge of singing pedagogy, number of Sing Up training activities	117
Appendix XIX: ANOVA - Knowledge of singing pedagogy, number of Sing Up training activities	119
One-way Analysis of Variance (ANOVA)	119
Post Hoc Tests	119
Appendix XX: Knowledge of musics, sex	120
Appendix XXI: Knowledge of musics, QTS	122
Appendix XXII: Knowledge of musics, number of Sing Up training activities	124
Appendix XXIII: ANOVA - Knowledge of musics, number of Sing Up training activities	126
One-way Analysis of Variance (ANOVA)	126
Post Hoc Tests	126
Appendix XXIV: The pupils in my group/class, sex	128
Appendix XXV: The pupils in my group/class, QTS	130
Appendix XXVI: The pupils in my group/class, number of Sing Up training activities	132
Appendix XXVII: My teaching/singing leadership, sex	134
Appendix XXVIII: My teaching/singing leadership, QTS	136
Appendix XXIX: My teaching/singing leadership, number of Sing Up training activities	138

List of figures

Figure 1: Respondents' age groups (Total)	14
Figure 2: Respondents' age-groups (SAGE 1)	16
Figure 3: Respondents' age-groups (SAGE 2)	16
Figure 4 Respondents' age-groups (SAGE 3)	17
Figure 5: Respondents' reported qualifications in Music/Singing	18
Figure 6: Possession of Qualified Teacher Status	19
Figure 7: Respondents' plans to undertake study for a Masters in Teaching & Learning or other formal award (introduced in SAGE 3)	20
Figure 8: Year-groups lead (SAGE 1, SAGE 2, SAGE 3)	21
Figure 9: Status in school (SAGE 3 only)	23
Figure 10: Mean score of singing self efficacy and number of Sing Up training activities	28
Figure 11: Boxplot of scores of singing self efficacy and number of Sing Up training activities	29
Figure 12: Mean score of knowledge of learners and number of Sing Up training activities	32
Figure 13: Boxplot of scores for knowledge of learners and number of Sing Up training activities	33
Figure 14: Mean rating of knowledge of singing pedagogy and number of Sing Up training activities	38
Figure 15: Respondents' qualifications in Music/Singing (SAGE 1)	84
Figure 16: Respondents' qualifications in Music/Singing (SAGE 2)	85
Figure 17: Respondents' qualifications in Music/Singing (SAGE 3)	85
Figure 18: Do you hold Qualified Teacher Status? (SAGE 1)	86
Figure 19: Do you hold Qualified Teacher Status? (SAGE 2)	87
Figure 20: Do you hold Qualified Teacher Status? (SAGE 3)	87
Figure 21: Respondents' formal responsibility for music at school (SAGE 1)	96

Figure 22: Respondents' formal responsibility for music at school (SAGE 2)   96
Figure 23: Respondents' formal responsibility for music at school (SAGE 3)   97
Figure 24: Local Authority representation (SAGE 1)   103
Figure 25: Local Authority representation (SAGE 2)   104
Figure 26: Local Authority representation (SAGE 3)   104

List of tables

Table 1: Distribution of responses by age phase   14
Table 2: Proportion of respondents with formal responsibility for music   22
Table 3: Local authorities and numbers of responses   24
Table 4: Singing self efficacy statistics overall   27
Table 5: Descriptive statistics, Knowledge of Learners   30

Introduction

The Institute of Education (IoE), University of London was invited to undertake an external evaluation of the Sing Up workforce development experience that was complimentary to, but separate from, the Sage Gateshead's own internal evaluation processes. The IoE evaluation made use of a specially designed, online instrument that examined Sing Up's perceived impact on two main aspects of professional development: (i) participants' 'singing self-efficacy' – their self perceptions of their own singing abilities; and (ii) their 'knowledge about singing' in three sub-areas (related to children's singing development, pedagogy – the teaching and learning of singing with children, and the choice of an appropriate singing repertoire).

Each section used a 7-point Likert scale which required participants to signal the extent to which they agreed/disagreed with statements about themselves and singing. These statements drew on existing findings in published literature. It was estimated that responding to the various statements would take up to 10 minutes. Although the original intention was for participants to complete the instrument both before and after their workforce development experience, this was not always possible due to constraints on their time. Thus the majority of responses were gathered after participants' had experience of the Sing Up programme.

Data were completed online and submitted direct to our server at the IoE for data collation and analyses. The text below presents a synthesis of the main findings from the cumulative data collection over a three year period (2007-2010)[1].

In addition to the closed questions which sought agreement on a 7-point scale, there were also opportunities for respondents to comment on open questions. The data from these form the second section of this report.

---

[1] Where it has been necessary to differentiate between these three years of data collection, the first year of the workforce development (i.e., from late 2007 through to the summer of 2008) is referred to as SAGE 1, the second year (i.e. the academic year from autumn 2008 to the summer of 2009) as SAGE 2, with the third year of workforce development (i.e. autumn 2009 to autumn 2010) as SAGE 3.

Respondents' demographic data

Research strands

The complete dataset comprises 1046 sets of responses[2]. Of these, 172 responses (16.4%) were collected during SAGE 1 (2007-2008), 223 responses (21.3%) were collected during SAGE 2 (2008-2009) and, finally, 651 responses (62.2%) were collected during SAGE 3 (the third year of this research evaluation, 2009-2010).

	Frequency	Percent	Valid Percent	Cumulative Percent
SAGE 1	172	16.4	16.4	16.4
SAGE 2	223	21.3	21.3	37.8
SAGE 3	651	62.2	62.2	100.0
Total	1046	100.0	100.0	

Respondents' sex

As expected, there is a large sex bias in the responses dataset. Almost nine in ten respondents (89.3%) were female. This is in line with staffing ratios in Primary schools as reported in national statistics:

> "In both nursery and primary schools, 85 per cent of full-time teachers were female in 2004/05. In secondary schools there was less difference between the sexes – 56 per cent of full-time teachers were female."[3]

---

[2] the actual number of participants was 947 (99 individuals responded twice during SAGE 1)
[3] http://www.statistics.gov.uk/cci/nugget.asp?id=1765 (accessed 20 October 2010)

The fact that the percentage of female respondents is slightly above the mean reported in the official statistics regarding the Primary school sector staffing bias is further also partially explained by research literature that suggests that women are much likelier to participate in surveys (both online and offline)[4].

	Frequency	Percent	Valid Percent	Cumulative Percent
Prefer not to say	28	2.7	2.7	2.7
Female	934	89.3	89.3	92.0
Male	84	8.0	8.0	100.0
Total	1046	100.0	100.0	

Respondents' age-groups

Of the 1046 participants across all three strands of the evaluation process (SAGE 1, SAGE 2, SAGE 3), approximately 13% were aged between 20 and 29 years, 19% were aged between 30 and 39 years, 35% were aged between 40 and 49 years and 30% were aged above 50 years (see Figure 1). Overall, nearly two thirds of the participant population were above the age of 40, suggesting that the Sing Up workforce development programme was particularly successful in reaching an age group that are reported to be somewhat resistant to such opportunities and less open to the possibilities of change in their professional practice[5]. A very small percentage (2.58%, n=27) did not provide information regarding their age.

---

[4] see among others: Sax, L.J., Gilmartin, S.K. & Bryant, A.N. (2003) Assessing response rates and nonresponse bias in web and paper surveys. *Research in Higher Education.* Vol 44 (4), pp. 409-432.
[5] Day, C., Sammons, P., Stobart, G., Kington, A., & Gu, Q. (2007). *Teachers Matter: Connecting Work, Lives and Effectiveness.* Maidenhead, Berks: Open University Press.

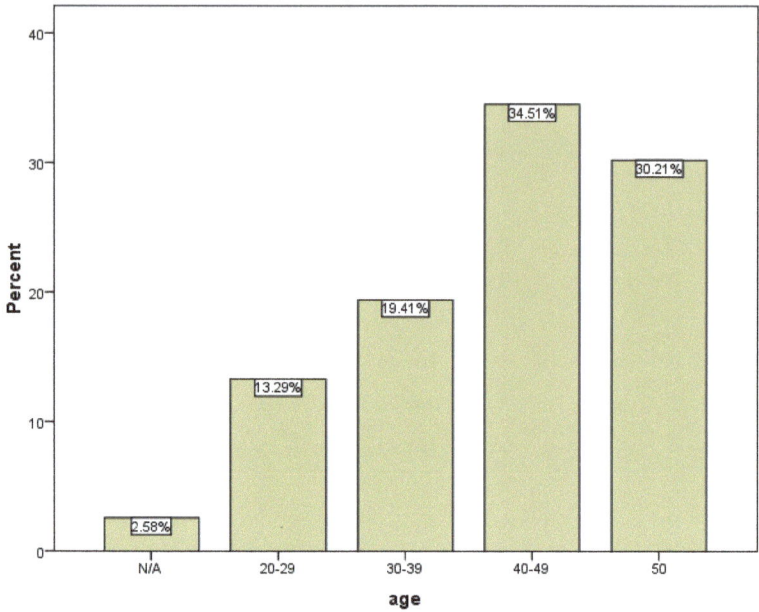

Figure 1: Respondents' age groups (Total)

Table 1: Distribution of responses by age phase

	Frequency	Percent	Valid Percent	Cumulative Percent
N/A	27	2.6	2.6	2.6
20-29	139	13.3	13.3	15.9
30-39	203	19.4	19.4	35.3
40-49	361	34.5	34.5	69.8
50	316	30.2	30.2	100.0
Total	1046	100.0	100.0	

The overall age-group distribution is mainly governed by the third strand of this research evaluation (SAGE 3) that counts for nearly two thirds of the respondent population. Differences were noted in the distribution patterns of participants' age-groups across the three research strands; particularly SAGE 1, where all age-groups appear to contribute approximately between 20 and 30 percent (see the three figures that follow, Figures 2, 3 and 4). This implies that older and more experienced adults (teachers, musicians) were attracted to the programme as it rolled out across the country,

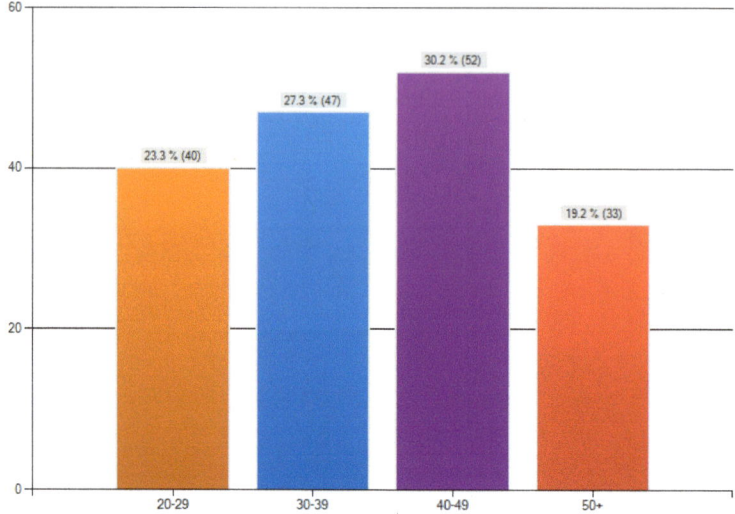

Figure 2: Respondents' age-groups (SAGE 1)

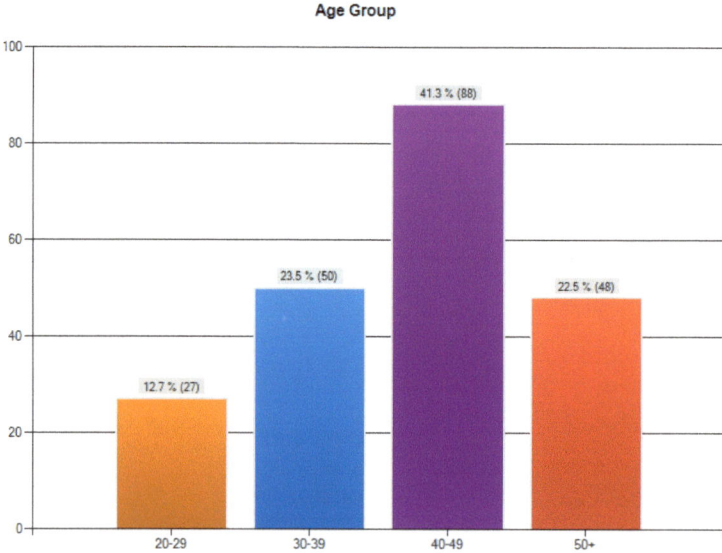

Figure 3: Respondents' age-groups (SAGE 2)

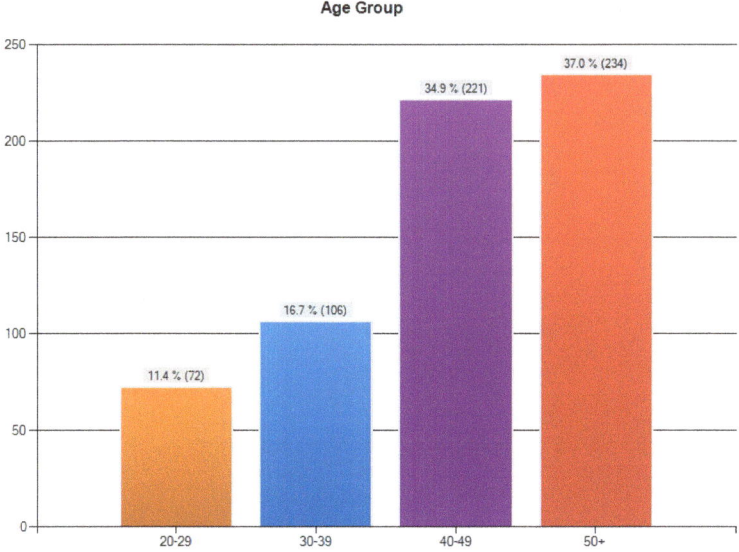

Figure 4 Respondents' age-groups (SAGE 3)

Respondents' qualifications in Music and/or Singing

Apart from 49 participants (4.7%) that did not provide an answer about whether they held a formal qualification in Music and/or singing, the respondent population was almost dichotomous: 479 participants (45.8%) reported that they did not hold a qualification (at the time of survey) and 518 participants (49.55%) reported that they did (Figure 5). As expected, the nature of the reported qualifications varied, but mainly referred to undergraduate degrees in Music and Graded (Associated Board) music examination certificates. A comprehensive list of all reported qualifications can be found at the end of this report (Appendix I: List of reported qualifications in Music and/or Singing, p73).

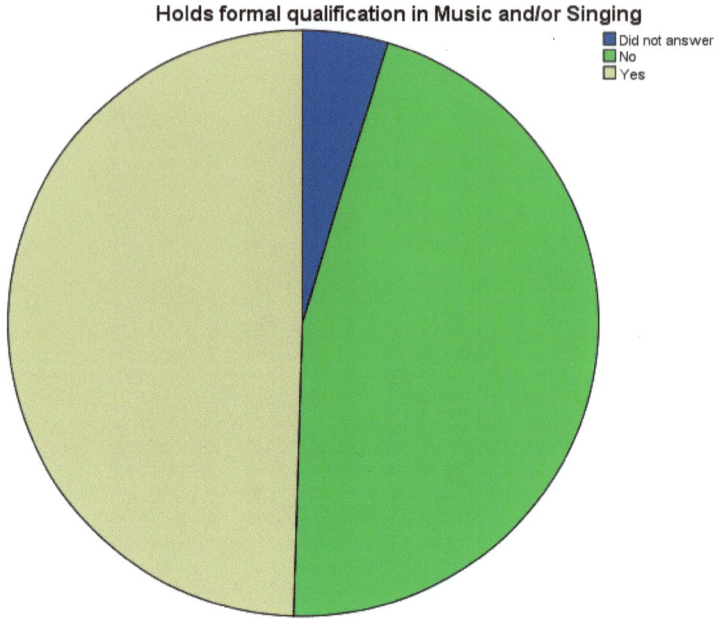

Figure 5: Respondents' reported qualifications in Music/Singing

More detail regarding the respondents' qualifications across the three research strands can be found within Appendix II.

Qualified teacher's status

More than two-thirds (70%, n=727) of all respondents reported that they held QTS (qualified teacher status). Of those holding QTS, slightly more than half (55%) had obtained it within the past ten years.

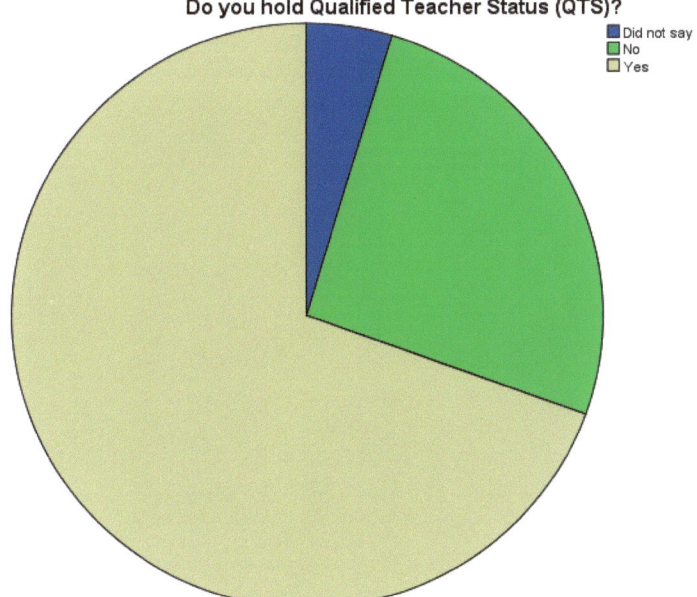

Figure 6: Possession of Qualified Teacher Status

More information regarding how these percentages vary between the three research strands can be found within Appendix III.

Masters in Teaching & Learning

In 2009-2010, the research team introduced a new question in the online research instrument, following a request from the SAGE Gateshead. All SAGE 3 respondents were asked whether they were considering embarking upon a "Masters in Teaching & Learning" programme (a new government-funded practice-based masters programme) or other formal award. The respondents had three options to choose from (Yes, Possibly, No). A free text-box was also included for providing information about 'other formal awards' that they might have been considering.

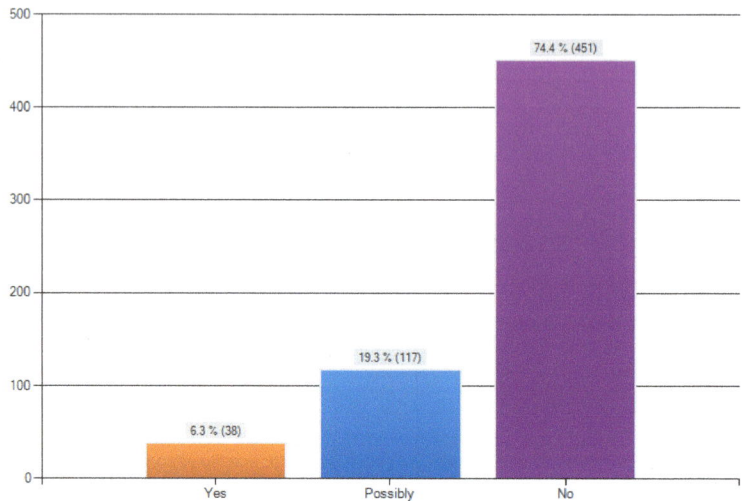

Figure 7: Respondents' plans to undertake study for a Masters in Teaching & Learning or other formal award (introduced in SAGE 3)

As is clear in the above figure (Figure 7), almost three in four participants (74.4%) reported that they were not considering studying for a 'Masters in Teaching & Learning' award. One in five participants (19.3%) stated that this was a possibility and 38 participants (6.3%) reported that they were considering this professional development pathway. Of those that provided a response in the open text-field, the majority mentioned that they already had a post-graduate qualification. A complete list of responses is provided within Appendix IV.

Pupil (student) age groups being lead or taught

Respondents were asked to report with which year group(s) they normally lead (or taught) singing. The possible categories included the main research focus (Primary-aged children), but also included Early Years through to Adulthood.

Respondents were given the chance to 'tick as many' options as appropriate. The results for each strand demonstrate that most participants provided singing leadership to more than one year (age) group, although the majority were within Key Stages 1 and 2 (ages 5+ to 10+ years).

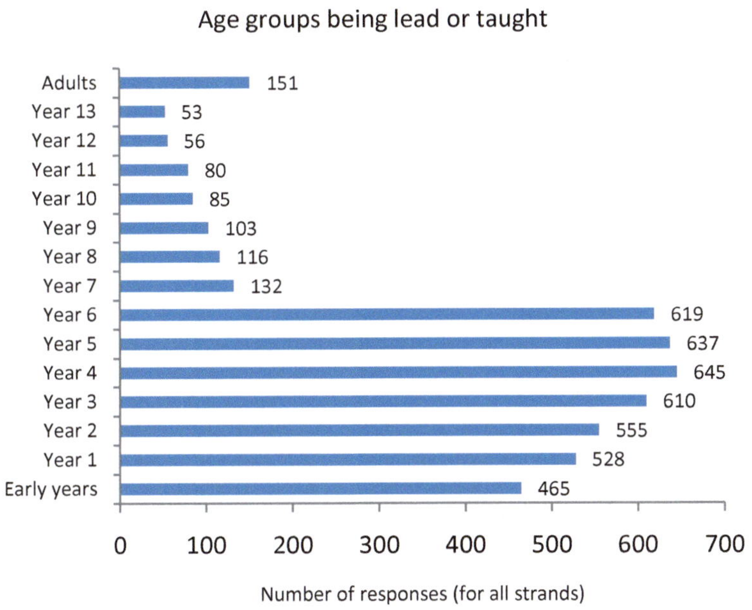

Age groups being lead or taught

Year group	Number of responses
Adults	151
Year 13	53
Year 12	56
Year 11	80
Year 10	85
Year 9	103
Year 8	116
Year 7	132
Year 6	619
Year 5	637
Year 4	645
Year 3	610
Year 2	555
Year 1	528
Early years	465

Number of responses (for all strands)

Figure 8: Year-groups lead (SAGE 1, SAGE 2, SAGE 3)

Among 'any other groups' (provided by the respondents in a special 'comments' field) were groups with learning disabilities, . The complete list of responses is available within Appendix V (page 89).

Formal responsibility for music in participants' schools

Respondents were asked to report whether they held some kind of formal responsibility for music in their schools. This question was extended in SAGE 3 with a request for more specific information about that responsibility. The available options were: teacher; governor; parent/guardian; classroom assistant/TA; visiting community musician or other.

Table 2: Proportion of respondents with formal responsibility for music

	Frequency	Percent	Cumulative Percent
Did not say	125	12.0	12.0
No	329	31.5	43.4
Yes	592	56.6	100.0
Total	1046	100.0	

The majority of respondents across all three years of data collection (n=592, 56.6%) reported holding some kind of formal responsibility for music in their schools (Table 2). This proportion shifted across the three years of the research. In the first year, the majority of the respondents (n=95, 60.1%) reported themselves *not* to hold a formal responsibility. Whereas in the third year, n=431, 71% of the respondents reported that they did. It can be hypothesized that this shift may derive from a gradual realisation by more people that participation in the SAGE Gateshead workforce development experience would be beneficial, irrespective of whether or not they already held a formal responsibility for music in their schools. A related factor may be evidenced in the shift in participant age grouping across the three years reported earlier, i.e., the increased numbers of older participants in 2009-2010 brought a concomitant likelihood that such a group would already have a music responsibility in their school (see *Respondents' age-groups*, p. 13 concerning the gradual increase of participants' age).

Respondents that used the 'other' option provided in the online response form mainly reported being Music and/or Arts coordinators. A full list of responses as well as figures that portray respondents' reported responsibilities across the three research strands are available within Appendix VI (p. 92).

Finally, the vast majority of SAGE 3 participants (n=358, 85.9%) reported that they were 'teachers' in their schools. Smaller groupings of 'classroom assistants/TAs' and 'visiting community musicians' were identically proportioned (n=6.2%, n=26, per group) (Figure 9).

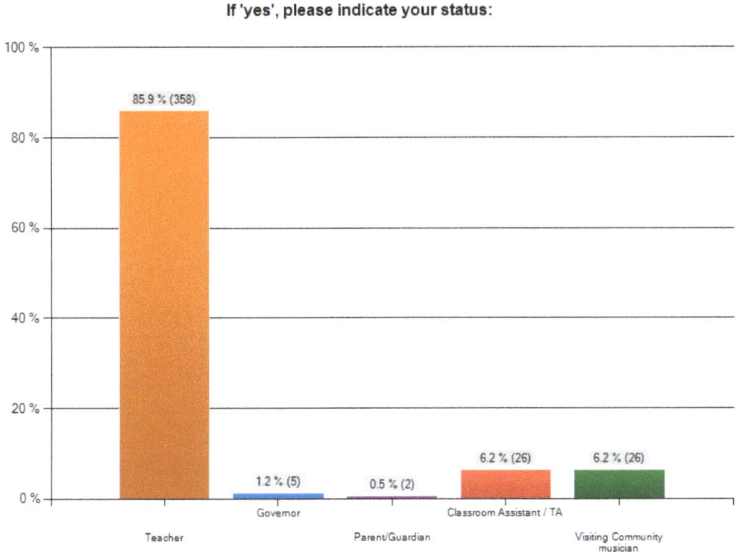

Figure 9: Status in school (SAGE 3 only)

Local authority

Respondents were asked to provide information about the local authorities in which they worked. Analyses of the response data demonstrated that all local authorities in England (formerly 'LEAs' or Local Education Authorities) were mentioned at least once. Nevertheless, of all 130 local authorities, 20 (15%) are mentioned in almost half of all responses (50.05%).

The following table provides information about the 22 most represented LAs[6] (Table 3). The complete list can be found within Appendix VII (p. 98).

Table 3: Local authorities and numbers of responses

Local authority	Number of responses	Percentage of total
Bristol City Council	38	4.09%
Stoke-on-Trent City Council	37	3.98%
North Yorkshire County Council	35	3.77%
Bradford City Council	27	2.91%
Cornwall County Council	26	2.80%
Kent County Council	26	2.80%
Kirklees Metropolitan Borough Council	25	2.69%
Hampshire County Council	25	2.69%
Suffolk County Council	24	2.58%
Cumbria County Council	24	2.58%
York City Council	23	2.48%
NOT APPLICABLE	20	2.15%
Cambridgeshire County Council	19	2.05%
Leicestershire County Council	18	1.94%
Norfolk County Council	17	1.83%
East Sussex County Council	17	1.83%
Hertfordshire County Council	17	1.83%
Derbyshire County Council	16	1.72%
Brighton and Hove City Council	16	1.72%
Durham County Council	15	1.61%
Devon County Council	15	1.61%
Birmingham City Council	15	1.61%

Additional information regarding the most represented LAs across the three research strands can be found within Appendix VIII (p. 103).

---

[6] This table includes 22 local authorities rather than 20 because Durham County Council, Devon County Council and Birmingham County Council are equally represented (n=15, 1.61%)

Internal consistency of the survey

As described within the introductory section, following the provision of demographic and background information, the participants were asked to signal the extent to which they agreed/disagreed with statements about themselves and singing. These statements were drawn from established research literature and related published data. There were 72 statements in total, divided into six sub-themes. These were:

heading	number of statements
Singing-related activities	17
Knowledge of Learners	7
Knowledge of Singing Pedagogy	11
Knowledge of Musics	8
The pupils in my group/class	19
My teaching/singing leadership	10

Post hoc statistical analyses of the responses suggested that the complete corpus of responses to the statements appeared to be highly consistent internally (Crombach's $\alpha = 0.940$, based on 848 [81.1%] valid cases).

Partial internal consistencies per heading were also computed and were also found to be very high[7].

heading	Crombach's α
Singing-related activities	.434
Knowledge of Learners	.852
Knowledge of Singing Pedagogy	.912
Knowledge of Musics	.901
The pupils in my group/class	.950
My teaching/singing leadership	.883

---

[7] This is evident for all sub-headings besides the first (singing related activities), where the rather low Crombach's α measure (.434) is likely to be due to the overall positive attitudes that the respondents demonstrated regarding their singing related activities.

Participants' singing self-efficacy

The participants were asked to respond on a number of Likert-type 7-point rating scales to indicate their agreement/disagreement with a set of 17 statements. These statements were:

> When I plan a singing activity, I am certain I can complete it successfully
>
> One of my problems is that I cannot get down to practising or rehearsing singing when I should
>
> If I can't sing something at first, I keep trying until I can
>
> When I set important goals for my singing activities, I rarely achieve them
>
> I give up on things before completing them
>
> I avoid facing difficult situations in my singing activities
>
> If a piece of music looks or sounds complicated, I will not even attempt to perform it
>
> When I have something unpleasant to do, I stick to it until I finish it
>
> When I decide to do something, I do it straight away
>
> When trying out a new piece of music, I soon give up if I am not initially successful
>
> If something unexpected happens when I sing, I do not handle it well
>
> I avoid pieces of music that look or sound too difficult for me
>
> Failure in a singing activity just makes me try harder
>
> I feel insecure about my singing
>
> I am a self-reliant singer
>
> I give up singing activities easily
>
> I do not seem capable of dealing with most problems that come up in my singing activities

All individual ratings were combined in order to contribute to a mean *singing self-efficacy score*. The maximum possible theoretical score is 7 (denoting an extremely positive self view of personal singing abilities), and the minimum possible theoretical score is 1 (denoting an extremely negative view). Consequently, if a participant generated an individual rating or composite score close to 4, this can be perceived to be a relatively neutral response.

Table 4: Singing self efficacy statistics overall

Descriptive Statistics					
	N	Minimum	Maximum	Mean	Std. Deviation
Singing self efficacy	930	1.5882	7.0000	5.400886	.9378666
Valid N (listwise)	930				

Overall, as can be seen by the above table, the results are relatively positive. The mean Singing self efficacy score for n=930 respondents was 5.4.

This appears to be evident for both male (mean=5.4, standard deviation=0.8, standard error=0.09) and female (mean=5.4, standard deviation=0.9, standard error=0.03) participants. The complete table of descriptive statistics can be found in Appendix IX (p. 105).

The same pattern is evident for both respondent group categories that either hold a qualified teacher status (QTS) or not (see Appendix X, p. 106).

Furthermore, the mean score of singing self efficacy appears to be closely linked to the number of Sing Up sessions/activities that the participants had attended (Figures 10 and 11).

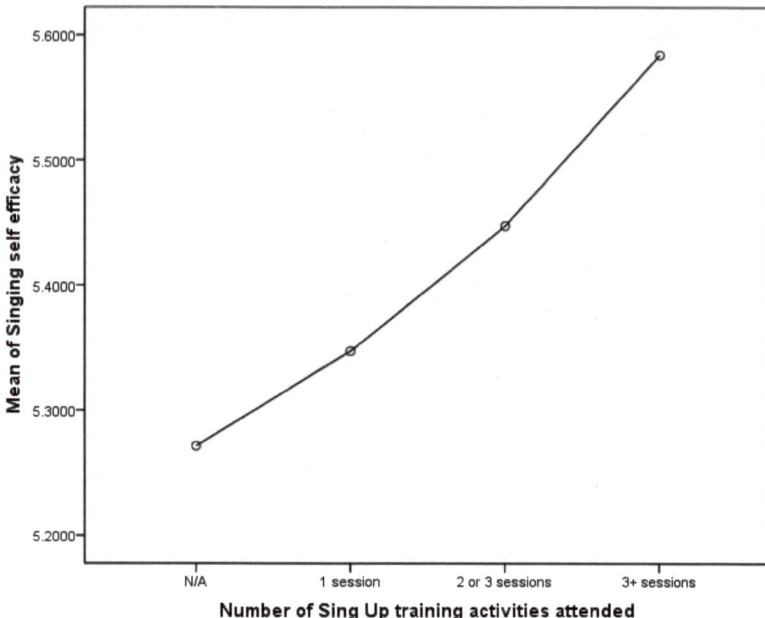
Figure 10: Mean score of singing self efficacy and number of Sing Up training activities

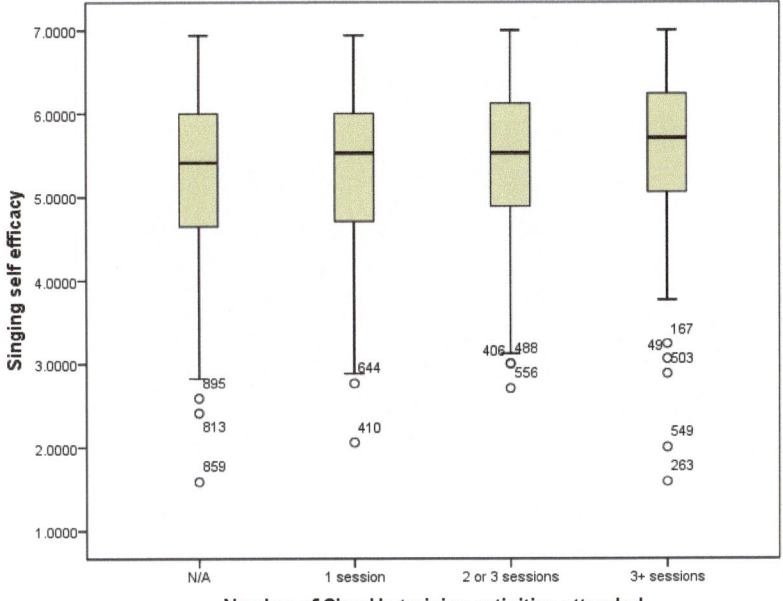

Figure 11: Boxplot of scores of singing self efficacy and number of Sing Up training activities

Although the difference in mean score is small (i.e. not 'significant' statistically), the data analyses demonstrate that respondents appear to be more positive and feel better about themselves as singers in relation to the (increasing) number of training sessions that they had attended (also see Appendix XI, p. 107 for a comprehensive table of descriptive statistics).

As expected, participants that had reported holding some kind of formal responsibility for teaching music/singing in school(s) appeared to be more positive (mean=5.6, standard deviation=0.8, standard error=0.04) compared to the participants that reported not holding a formal responsibility (mean=4.98, standard deviation=1.01, standard error=0.06)[8].

---

[8] This difference was statistically significant: $F(2, 927)=47.688$, $p=.000$

Knowledge of learners

The participants were asked to use a number of Likert-type 7-point rating scales in order to indicate their agreement/disagreement with a set of seven statements. These statements were:

> I am a good role model
>
> I understand vocal development
>
> I understand vocal development and I can plan teaching and learning in singing
>
> I take account of how children use singing to define their culture
>
> I take account of the learning that children bring from other contexts
>
> I provide children with the opportunity to lead singing
>
> I involve parents and other members of the community in singing

All individual ratings were combined in order to contribute to a mean *knowledge of learners score*. The maximum possible theoretical score is 7 (denoting an extremely positive view), and the minimum possible theoretical score is 1 (denoting an extremely negative view). Consequently, respondents achieving a score close to 4 were perceived to be neutral/moderate regarding their self-reported knowledge of learners.

Table 5: Descriptive statistics, Knowledge of Learners

Descriptive Statistics	N	Minimum	Maximum	Mean	Std. Deviation
Knowledge of Learners	917	1.2857	7.0000	4.905904	1.1160511
Valid N (listwise)	917				

Respondents appeared to be somewhat positive on average. The mean knowledge of learners score was 4.9 (n=917) (Table 5).

This appears to be evident for both male (mean=5.08, standard deviation=1.04, standard error=0.11) and female participants (mean=4.88, standard deviation=0.9, standard error=1.12). The complete table of descriptive statistics can be found in Appendix XII (p. 109)

No significant difference is also apparent between respondents in relation to whether they held qualified teacher status (QTS) or not (see Appendix XIII, p.110).

Nevertheless, despite the relative neutrality overall, the same pattern that was observed in the previous section is also apparent here: that is, respondents that participated in more Sing Up training sessions reported greater confidence in their (mean) knowledge of learners (Figures 12 and 13).

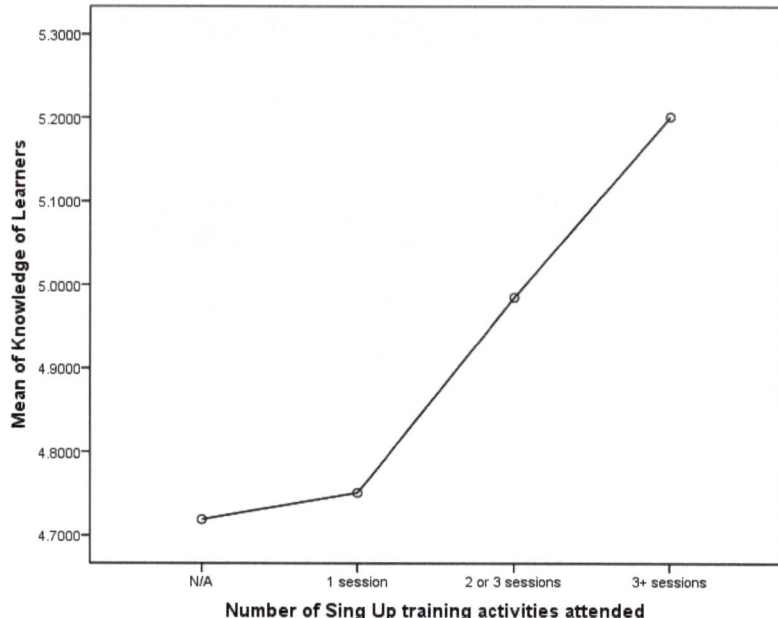

Figure 12: Mean score of knowledge of learners and number of Sing Up training activities

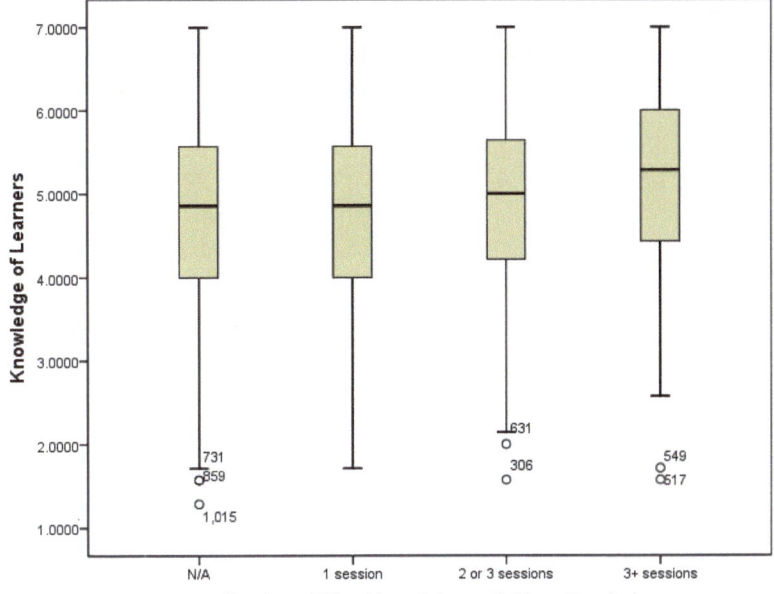

Figure 13: Boxplot of scores for knowledge of learners and number of Sing Up training activities

A comprehensive table containing descriptive statistics regarding the mean *knowledge of learners* scores and the number of Sing Up training activities attended can be found in Appendix XIV (p. 111).

These differences are also statistically significant, as there was a significant effect of the number of Sing Up training sessions on knowledge of learners mean scores at the $p<.05$ level for the four categories [$F(3, 913) = 10.74$, $p = 0.000$][9].

Finally, participants that had reported holding some kind of formal responsibility for teaching music/singing in school(s) appeared to be more positive regarding their knowledge of learners (mean=5.1, standard deviation=1.02, standard

---

[9] A one-way analysis of variance statistical method was employed. See Appendix XV (p. 58) for a more detailed overview.

error=0.13) compared to the participants that reported not holding a formal responsibility (mean=4.48, standard deviation=1.17, standard error=0.07)[10].

---

[10] This difference was statistically significant: $F(2, 914)=32.568$, $p=.000$

Knowledge of Singing Pedagogy

The participants were asked to use a number of Likert-type 7-point rating scales in order to indicate their agreement/disagreement with a set of 11 statements. These statements were:

> I am able to promote vocal health and function
>
> I am able to address basic singing issues
>
> I am able to promote and support high quality singing performances
>
> I am able to establish a 'safe' environment for singing
>
> I am able to promote varied performing opportunities
>
> I am able to differentiate teaching strategies to meet individual and group needs in singing
>
> I am able to integrate singing into other musical activities
>
> I am able to extend vocal use in non-conventional ways
>
> I am able to use ICT to support the creative use of the voice
>
> I am able to draw on singers and singing leaders from the wider musical community
>
> I am able to encourage cultural exchange and diversity in singing

All individual ratings were combined in order to contribute to a mean *knowledge of singing pedagogy score*. The maximum possible theoretical score is 7 (denoting an extremely positive view/attitude), and the minimum possible theoretical score is 1 (denoting an extremely negative view/attitude). Consequently, respondents achieving a score close to 4 were perceived to be neutral/moderate regarding their self-reported knowledge of singing pedagogy.

Descriptive Statistics

	N	Minimum	Maximum	Mean	Std. Deviation
Knowledge of Singing Pedagogy	1046	1.0000	7.0000	4.864045	1.154471
Valid N (listwise)	1046				

Although at a first glance, the respondents appear to be almost neutral (n=1046, mean score = 4.86), in reality, the responses are skewed to the right (more positive). The fact that the responses were not distributed normally (see figure 14) was verified by a One-Sample Kolmogorov-Smirnov Test (N=890, Asymptotic Sig.=.048).

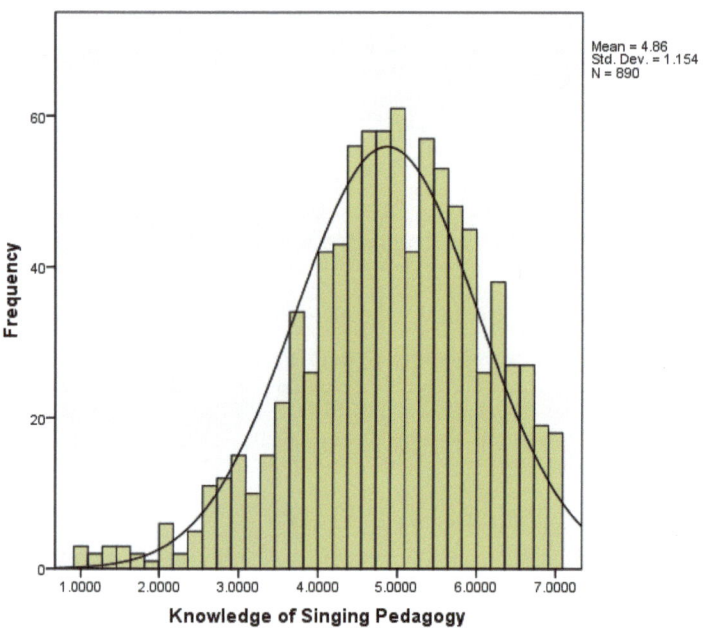

Figure 14: Knowledge of Singing Pedagogy, histogram

There is a slight difference between male and female respondents. Male respondents appear to be slightly more confident regarding their knowledge of singing pedagogy (mean= 4.6, standard deviation= 0.2) compared to female respondents (mean= 4.16, standard deviation= 0.065). This may reflect the likelihood that males have a reported tendency to report themselves as more confident in undertaking tasks[11,12]. The complete table of descriptive statistics can be found in Appendix XVI (p. 115).

There is a statistically significant difference between respondents that reported holding qualified teacher status (QTS) compared to those that did not. As might be expected, perhaps, given the focus in the set of questions on pedagogy, respondents holding QTS were more positive (mean= 4.43, standard deviation= 1.78) as opposed to non-qualified teachers (mean=3.95, standard deviation= 2.14), although it should be noted that both means are around the relatively neutral score of 4. A comprehensive table with descriptive statistics is available within Appendix XVII (p. 116).

Once again, it is notable that the same experiential pattern that was observed in the previous section is also apparent here: the more that respondents participated in Sing Up training sessions, the greater their knowledge of singing pedagogy mean rating (Figure 15).

---

[11] Zimmermann, B.J. and Martinez-Pons, M. (1990). 'Student Differences in Self- Regulated Learning: Relating Grade, Sex, and Giftedness to Self-Efficacy and Strategy Use', Journal of Educational Psychology 82(1), 51–59.

[12] Nielsen, S.G. (2004). Strategies and self-efficacy beliefs in instrumental and vocal individual practice: a study of students in higher music education. *Psychology of Music, 32*(4), 418-431.

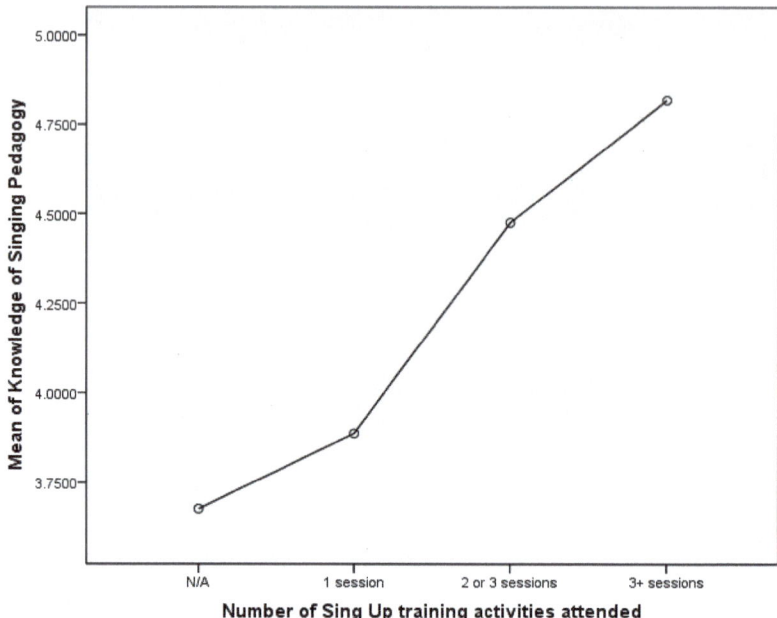

Figure 15: Mean rating of knowledge of singing pedagogy and number of Sing Up training activities

Unsurprisingly, participants that had reported holding some kind of formal responsibility for teaching music/singing in school(s) appeared to be more positive regarding their knowledge of singing pedagogy (mean=5.1, standard deviation=1.00, standard error=0.42) compared to the participants that reported not holding a formal responsibility (mean=4.36, standard deviation=1.24, standard error=0.08)[13].

---

[13] This difference was statistically significant: $F(2, 887)=40.963$, $p=.000$

Knowledge of Musics

The participants were also asked to use a number of Likert-type 7-point rating scales in order to indicate their agreement/disagreement with a set of 8 statements concerning song repertoire. These statements were:

> I am able to make informed and appropriate repertoire choices
>
> I know where to access support
>
> I am able to explore and understand the vocal implications of music from a wide range of genres and cultures
>
> I understand the role that singing plays in different cultures
>
> I am able to draw on musical genre-specific expertise from the wider musical community
>
> I understand the importance of the physical space in which singing takes place
>
> I lead and conduct singing groups
>
> I celebrate local, regional and national musics

All individual ratings were combined in order to contribute to a mean *knowledge of musics*. The maximum possible theoretical score is 7 (denoting an extremely positive view/attitude), and the minimum possible theoretical score is 1 (denoting an extremely negative view/attitude). Consequently, respondents achieving a score close to 4 were perceived to be neutral/moderate regarding their self-reported knowledge of musics.

Descriptive Statistics

	N	Minimum	Maximum	Mean	Std. Deviation
Knowledge of Musics	881	1.000	7.000	5.07179	1.223406
Valid N (listwise)	881				

As can be seen from the above table, there is an overall bias in the mean towards a positive belief in participants' knowledge of appropriate singing repertoire for children. This is a welcome outcome, given the tendency for the majority of participants to have experience of teaching in Primary schools.

There is no significant difference between respondents that reported holding qualified teacher status (QTS) as opposed to those that did not. A comprehensive table with descriptive statistics is available within Appendix XXI (p. 122).

In line with what was presented within the previous sections, participants that had reported holding some kind of formal responsibility for teaching music/singing in school(s) appeared to be more positive regarding their knowledge of musics (mean=5.32, standard deviation=1.09, standard error=0.46) to the participants that reported not holding a formal responsibility (mean=4.53, standard deviation=1.27, standard error=0.07)[14].

Respondents that participated in more Sing Up training sessions reported greater confidence in their mean knowledge of musics scores.

---

[14] This difference was statistically significant: $F(2, 878)=40.860, p=.000$

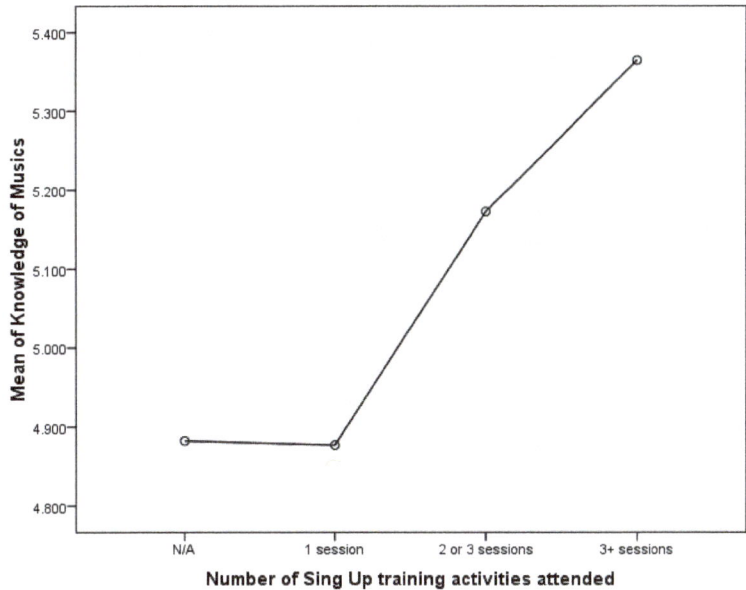

Figure 16: Mean score of knowledge of musics and number of Sing Up training activities

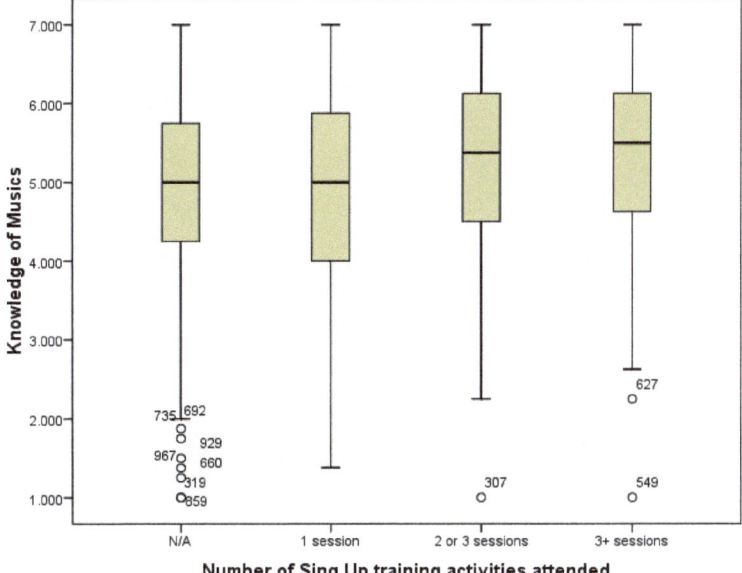

Figure 17: Boxplot of scores for knowledge of musics and number of Sing Up training activities

A comprehensive table containing descriptive statistics regarding the mean knowledge of musics scores and the number of Sing Up training activities attended can be found in Appendix XXII (p. 124).

These differences are also statistically significant as there was a significant positive effect of the number of Sing Up training sessions on knowledge of musics mean scores at the p<.05 level for the four categories [$F(3, 877) = 9.140$, p = 0.000][15].

---

[15] A one-way analysis of variance statistical method was employed. See Appendix XXIII (p.115) for a more detailed overview.

The pupils in my group/class

The participants were asked to use a number of Likert-type 7-point rating scales in order to indicate their agreement/disagreement with a set of 19 statements. These statements were:

> the pupils in my group class:
> - enjoy their music lessons
> - enjoy singing
> - are confident in their music lessons
> - take part in extra-curricular musical activities
> - have a range of well developed musical skills
> - have a well developed range of strategies for composing
> - perform well
> - have well developed listening skills
> - love music
> - have positive attitudes towards music
> - are generally well behaved
> - are able to concentrate on their work
> - help each other
> - are on time for school
> - enjoy learning
> - are well motivated
> - generally have high levels of self-esteem
> - attend school regularly
> - are not involved in bullying

All individual ratings were combined in order to contribute to a mean *knowledge of pupils in my group/class* score. The maximum possible theoretical score is 7 (denoting an extremely positive view/attitude), and the minimum possible theoretical score is 1 (denoting an extremely negative view/attitude). Consequently, respondents achieving a score close to 4 were perceived to be neutral/moderate regarding their self-reported understanding of the pupils in their group/class.

Descriptive Statistics

	N	Minimum	Maximum	Mean	Std. Deviation
The Pupils in My Group/Class	867	1.0000	7.0000	5.518788	.9179178
Valid N (listwise)	867				

Overall, the respondents appear to be positive (n=867, mean score = 5.52).

There is no apparent difference between male and female respondents. Male respondents (mean= 5.53, standard deviation= 0.82) appeared to respond similarly to female respondents (mean= 5.52, standard deviation= 0.93). The complete table of descriptive statistics can be found in Appendix XXIV (p. 128).

As one might expect, there is a slightly more positive attitude demonstrated by respondents that reported holding qualified teacher status (QTS) as opposed to those that did not. A comprehensive table with descriptive statistics is available within Appendix XXV (p. 130).

Respondents that participated in 3+ Sing Up training sessions reported greater confidence in their mean knowledge of the pupils in their groups/classes, compared to participants that had attended fewer sessions.

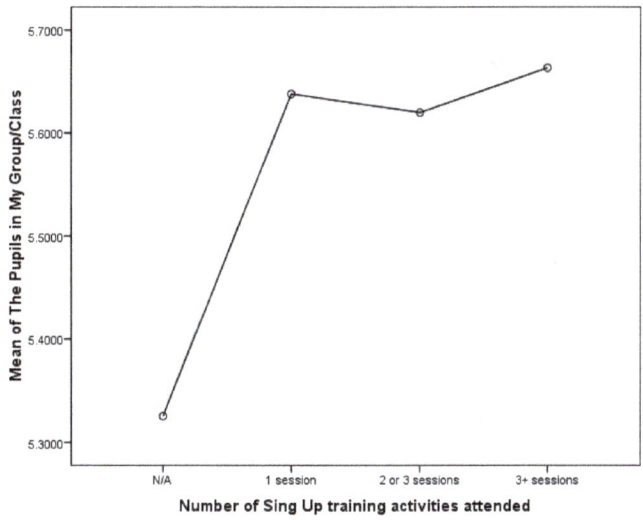

Figure 18: Mean score of knowledge of pupils in my group/class and number of Sing Up training activities

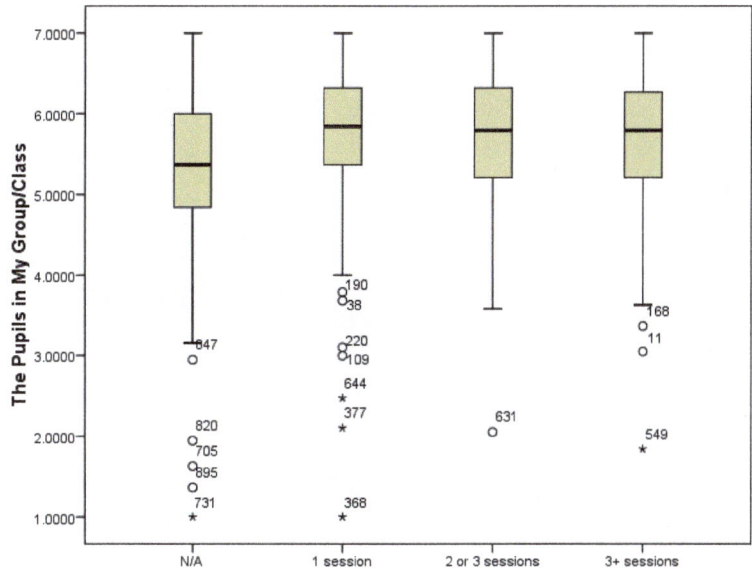

Figure 19: Boxplot of scores for knowledge of pupils in my group/class and number of Sing Up training activities

A comprehensive table containing descriptive statistics regarding the mean knowledge of pupils in my group/class scores and the number of Sing Up training activities attended can be found in Appendix XXVI (p. 132).

My teaching/singing leadership

The participants were asked to use a number of Likert-type 7-point rating scales in order to indicate their agreement/disagreement with a set of ten statements. These statements were:

> I am an effective teacher/leader
>
> Generally, I am confident about my teaching/leading
>
> I am confident about teaching music to my group/class
>
> I enjoy teaching/leading music to my group/class
>
> I am confident about teaching/leading singing to my group/class
>
> I am confident that I can sing well enough to teach/lead my group/class music
>
> I am able to read music
>
> I am able to play a musical instrument sufficiently well to use in music lessons
>
> I like teaching/leading music
>
> I think that specialist music teachers/leaders should teach/lead music in primary schools

All individual ratings were combined in order to contribute to a mean *teaching/singing leadership* score. The maximum possible theoretical score is 7 (denoting an extremely positive view/attitude), and the minimum possible theoretical score is 1 (denoting an extremely negative view/attitude). Consequently, respondents achieving a score close to 4 were perceived to be neutral/moderate regarding their self-reported teaching/singing leadership levels.

Descriptive Statistics

	N	Minimum	Maximum	Mean	Std. Deviation
My teaching/singing leadership	848	1.3000	7.0000	5.698821	1.0925630
Valid N (listwise)	848				

Overall, the respondents appear to be positive (n=848, mean score = 5.70).

There is a small difference between male and female respondents. Male respondents (mean= 5.86, standard deviation= 0.92) appeared to be more positive compared to female respondents (mean= 5.68, standard deviation= 1.10). The complete table of descriptive statistics can be found in Appendix XXIV (p. 128).

There is a slightly more positive attitude demonstrated by respondents that reported holding qualified teacher status (QTS) as opposed to those that did not. A comprehensive table with descriptive statistics is available within Appendix XXVIII (p. 136).

In line with what was presented throughout almost all of the previous headings, it is evident that respondents that participated in more Sing Up training sessions appeared to be more positive regarding their teaching/singing leadership.

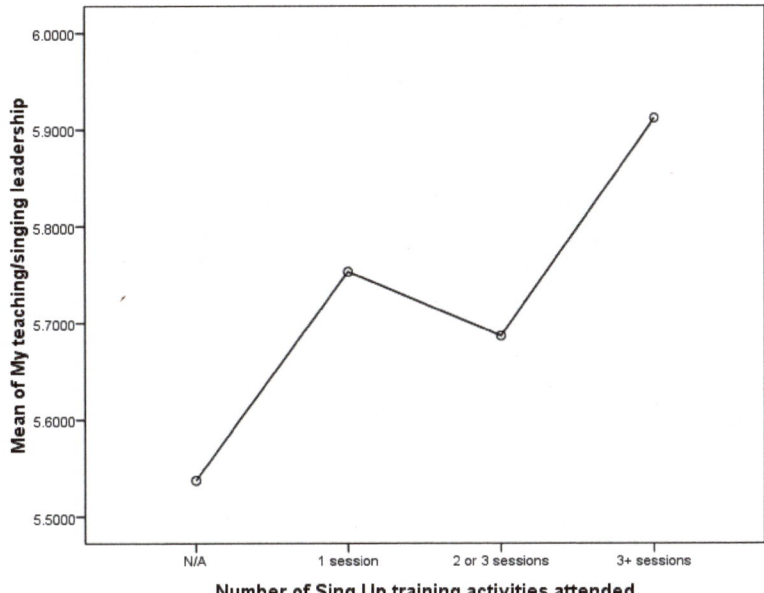

Figure 20: Mean score of teaching/singing leadership and number of Sing Up training activities

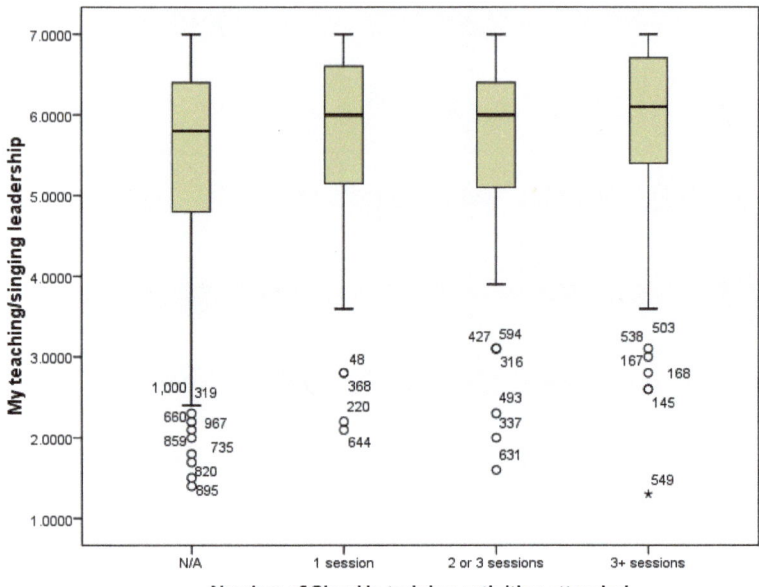

Figure 21: Boxplot teaching/singing leadership and number of Sing Up training activities

A comprehensive table containing descriptive statistics regarding the mean teaching/singing leadership scores and the number of Sing Up training activities attended can be found in Appendix XXIX (p. 138).

Qualitative data analyses

The following section seeks to illustrate the wide variety of responses given by teachers and vocal practitioners as part of the research. The views given represent respondents working with Sing Up materials in very different ways, from Sing Up area leaders and vocal practitioners leading workshops, to teaching staff in schools and lunchtime supervisors working in the playground. Responses have been brought together to illustrate the emerging themes shared across the divergent population and the potential differences in experiences, where they occur. In each case, an overview is given, that summarises an emergent theme, followed by more detailed section, including specific examples.

What changes have you seen in the children that you work with since receiving your *Sing Up* training?

Overview

In response to this question, the changes described fell into two main categories, that of the **size of change** and the **nature of the change**. For example, the **size of change** may refer to (i) those events witnessed at the individual level that were deeply significant for those concerned, or (ii) those experienced as part of an extended or larger group. Furthermore, the **nature of the change** varied, in some instances, observed changes were of (iii) a musical nature, whilst in others, responses described changes in (iv) other than musical behaviour such as emotional literacy, concentration or learning across the curriculum.

Detail

The **size of the change** observed ranged from those noted in individual pupils or teachers, across single classes, to the changes observed across community groups or whole school populations. On an individual level, one teacher reported that a child with special educational needs had approached her after a singing session, stood still, and then said, 'I LOVE that song, I LOVE all the songs' and walked away. The teacher added 'What other job would give you the feeling that did? I was delighted.' Another teacher described how a pupil had struggled to spell his own name. 'I worked out a simple song for him, and from that, he learned to spell his name.'

Some teachers reported that their classes were, as a result of the Sing Up initiatives, 'breaking into song during the day.' On a whole school level, one teacher stated 'Sing Up has opened the door to singing with my children at school. I can't thank you enough.' Another described how, in a recent OfSTED inspection, the 'exuberant singing in both class and assembly' had been praised. The improvement in singing, the teacher claimed, had 'happened since the introduction of the Sing Up initiatives.' A teacher told of how singing assemblies had positively impacted upon the pupils across the whole school, providing a 'sense of identity, community and belonging, as well as...lots of fun.'

In addition, the **nature of the change** observed varied widely. In some instances, observed changes were of a musical nature, whilst in others, responses described changes in behaviour, emotional literacy, concentration and learning across the curriculum.

Changes of a **musical nature** included comments such as 'posture is improved', 'quality of sound is improved', 'quality of singing [has] improved, especially note pitching', 'the quality of singing is better, they watch and listen more'. These comments would indicate that it is not only the quantity, but also the quality of singing that has improved. Pupils attitudes towards singing were also mentioned, describing how the 'children have a more positive attitude to singing', that they were 'keen to sing' and that singing was 'more readily accepted as 'cool' by a wider group of children, including the boys throughout the school.'

Changes in other areas of **social and emotional development** included the impact that 'singing leadership' had on pupils, who were 'empowered to lead by helping to hold harmony parts [and] remember lyrics.' Singing sessions enabled pupils to 'add their ideas and take responsibility' in a safe environment. Pupils were able to 'express themselves individually as a whole group.' Singing games 'helped children co-operate will in the playground' which, in turn, 'helped with social issues such as bullying at play time.'

Changes noted in **learning behaviours** included the response that 'concentration is better', whilst another teacher described how singing in the classroom setting enabled the pupils 'to calm down which...helped them concentrate on their work.' The use of singing in the classroom had supported the assimilation of information in other curriculum areas, as the 'children have also learnt so much through singing songs about geography, history [and] mathematics' through the use of the *Song Bank* had also provided a support strategy for the revision of new information, where pupils were seen 'using some of the songs to help...retrieve information.'

Neutral responses to the question tended to come from those teachers who felt that singing was already an established part of their school's life, for example 'we have always enjoyed singing and this was already a musical school' and 'we have always done lots of singing in school, singing is just natural here.' However, even in schools that had described themselves as already committed to singing, staff recognised that further changes and improvements had taken place, for example, 'we have always had a good singing ethos in the school, but I have seen children exceed expectations in…their singing.'

What changes in your own practice have you noticed since receiving training?

Overview

Responses to this question were broadly positive and seemed to fall into two main categories: the impact of the Sing Up training on (i) the **teachers' sense of self confidence as vocal leaders**, and (ii) the **provision of teaching materials to support the teaching of singing in schools**, including the provision of a **peer support network amongst fellow professionals.**

Detail

In terms of the **teachers' sense of self confidence as vocal leaders**, many of the responses to this question can be encapsulated within the following response; 'I am more confident at leading the group. I am less concerned when things go wrong (with them or me). It becomes an opportunity rather than a mistake!' Many teachers described how their confidence in their own singing voices, and their ability to teach singing had grown. 'I am more confident and will sing without a piano' stated one teacher, whilst another felt that the training had 'enabled me to sing reasonably confidently in class with the children.' One teacher described feeling 'a lot more confident with singing and music, and the teaching of it' and as a result, had begun to 'enjoy teaching [the pupil] these sessions.' A teacher who reported having 'grown in confidence' was now 'willing to tackle harder pieces, including part songs.' This willingness to push their own teaching practice was mirrored in the comments of another practitioner who said that the training had taught her how to 'stretch the children, to challenge them to develop.'

Many comments referred to the **provision of teaching materials to support the teaching of singing in schools.** One teacher described how she now knew 'where to access fresh ideas', while another praised how the song bank resources 'often link[ed] with topics and provide another opportunity to incorporate music [and] singing into the curriculum.' Others described the variety of available material as 'fantastic', praising the 'better repertoire, better teaching techniques [and] fun warm ups.'

In addition to the increased provision of teaching materials to support the teaching of singing, the increased accessibility of a **peer support network amongst fellow professionals** was mentioned by a number of respondents. Having felt professionally isolated, one teacher was pleased to have 'made contact with other teachers who [could] help and support' when needed. Another explained the importance of being able to 'engage in conversation with other professionals', including the opportunity to 'share with others, and learn from others.' In some circumstances, this increased professional collaboration had led to teachers working together to teach singing, evidenced by statements such as 'my team teaching skills have improved', whereas in others it provided informal supportive fora, where it was 'good to share ideas with other non-specialist teachers.'

Please offer some information regarding your own or your pupils' emotional experiences during singing?

Overview

Many of the respondents chose to give details of the emotional experiences of their pupils during singing, rather than themselves. Of these responses, there seemed to be two main areas of experience that were referred to. Firstly, that singing provided the possibility that all pupils (i) could **achieve on an equal level** with others and, within that, **engage or re-engage with learning through singing**. In addition, that singing provided (ii) the opportunity for pupils **to experience heightened emotions**. Further to the experience of heightened emotion, the respondents highlighted the need for **time and space for reflection** for both teachers and pupils alike.

Detail

Evidence that singing provided the opportunity for a wide variety of pupils to **achieve on an equal level with others** was provided by comments such as 'all children can be successful' in singing. One example of how singing enabled a pupil to communicate more successfully with their peers included the description from one teacher of how a pupil who had 'difficulty with [the] spoken word, when asked to speak on their own' had been able to 'find more courage' and 'sing a response.' The ability for all pupils to **engage or re-engage with learning through singing** was referred to in the statement 'the behaviour in our singing time is excellent, even from the more challenging pupils.' One teacher described how singing had 'engaged disaffected pupils' who had found something that they 'enjoy and feel part of on an equal level which sometimes in academic areas they do not.' This view was reflected in the responses of another teacher who had experienced some 'less academically able children' had 'engaged particularly well and their self esteem improved' as a result of singing.

In one school, pupils with special educational needs had gained 'confidence in particular from singing.' The teacher goes on to tell how 'it always amazes me that children who find learning generally difficult...are able to learn a huge repertoire of songs, word perfect and with confidence.' The impact of singing on the confidence of pupils was referred to by many of the respondents when answering this question. Some teachers reflected on how they had watched 'children's confidence grow' when they were singing solos. Singing was thought to have 'given children confidence and self-esteem.' There was frequent mention that singing, they felt, 'certainly raises self-esteem' and that participation in singing session had led to 'heightened self-esteem' amongst their pupils.

Singing was felt to provide pupils and teachers with a safe arena in which **to experience heightened emotions**. The effect of singing on the emotional well being of pupils was described by one teacher as 'they glow – [it is] very hard to explain, they give their absolute all and love working together.' Another described how the 'children concentrate, enjoy [and] try their best.' The children from one school were described as having an 'increased sense of well being and involvement when they sing as a group.' One teacher tells how the children have 'great big smiles on their faces' as they sing and that the pupils' energy created a 'real buzz in the room.'

Several respondents highlighted the need for **time and space for reflection** for both teachers and pupils alike. Teachers described how heightened emotions during singing sessions had reached such levels that the performance of 'some pieces of music move us to tears!' Another teacher reported that 'lots of children and teachers enjoy the singing sessions and feel uplifted. Sometimes songs can cause children to become tearful when singing.' In these circumstances, teachers suggested allowing 'reflection space after singing emotionally charged songs', making sure to notice 'the signals when people need a moment' and the importance of 'not making them feel... silly about reacting this way.'

Is singing important to you and the children that you work with?

Overview

From the responses gathered regarding the question of the 'importance of singing', many individuals gave detailed and impassioned statements. One interesting trend amongst the answers to this question was the tendency for respondents to refer to the whole community, be it a class, a school, a choir or the delegates of a workshop, rather than the individual or 'you and the children' as described above. A **heightened sense of community** was a dominant theme in many of the responses. Further references were made to the possibility that singing enabled all pupils to **achieve on an equal level** with others (as also found in responses to the question 'Please offer some information regarding you or your pupils' emotional experiences during singing?' above). Singing was also considered to be important as it impacted positively on the pupils' sense of **social and emotional development** (as also discussed in responses to the question 'What changes have you seen in the children that you work with since receiving your Sing Up training?' above).

Other responses touched on the possibility of **transferable skills** fostered within singing sessions that impacted on other areas of learning and life skills, such as discipline, memory and spatial awareness. In addition, the use of **singing as a learning tool** was considered.

Detail

The act of singing together was described by many as something that created a **heightened sense of community**. For example, 'it is the one thing in school we do that brings us all together' and 'when a group sing together...it helps the group bond and this in turn affects how they work together in other class situations.' The skills fostered and the experiences that the pupils shared in singing sessions were thought to extend beyond the end of the activities. Singing was described as being able to 'promote team work', 'collaboration', 'promote group cohesion' and 'facilitate co-operation in other areas.' Perhaps the most succinct description given was that singing was 'social glue.'[16]

Various aspects of **social and emotional development** were mentioned by respondents. Singing was thought to 'elevate our sense of well being', 'promote...individual emotional well being' with 'self esteem [going] through the roof' when pupils' efforts were 'encouraged and appreciated by their peers and other adults.' Singing was described as an activity that 'makes everyone feel valued.' Interestingly, some teachers reflected on how singing had offered them the 'opportunity to see another side of a pupil's character.'

Further reference was made to the possibility that singing enabled all pupils to **achieve on an equal level** with others. Singing provided an 'attainable, levelling group activity', in which all children were able to 'feel that they can shine.' Singing was an opportunity for pupils to 'take part in the same activity at various levels', enabling each to experience success. For some, singing facilitated 'talent, undiscovered in purely academic work.' Some teachers referred to the importance of the pupils' voice, where singing enabled 'less vocal children to make a valuable contribution', as well as 'break[ing] down language barriers.'

---

[16] For other recent research evidence to support this claim, see (1) Kirschner, S., & Tomasello, M. (2010). Joint music making promotes prosocial behaviour in 4-year-old children. *Evolution and Human Behaviour, 31*, 354-364; and (2) Welch, G.F., Himonides, E., Saunders, J., Papageorgi, I., Preti, C., Rinta, T., Vraka, M., Stephens Himonides, C., Stewart, C., Lanipekun, J., & Hill, J. (2010). *Researching the impact of the National Singing Programme 'Sing Up' in England: Main findings from the first three years (2007-2010). Children's singing development, self-concept and sense of social inclusion.* Institute of Education, University of London. [pp41]. There is a range of other research evidence to suggest that engagement in the arts can decrease anxiety and stress, as well as being likely to promote psychological and physical well-being and quality of life, e.g. Stuckey, H., & Nobel, J., (2010). The connection between art, healing and public health: a review of current literature. *American Journal of Public Health, 100*, 254-263.

Other responses touched on the possibility of **transferable skills** fostered within singing sessions that impacted on other areas of learning and life, such as related to discipline, memory and spatial awareness. Singing games were thought to 'improve spatial awareness and encourage friendships'. Learning songs was thought to 'develop the memory', as 'holding a song in your head helps with holding other information, like numbers in numeracy [and] mental maths.' Singing was also thought to strengthen the 'development of musical literacy' and 'improve listening skills.'

Singing as a learning tool was considered to be important by a number of respondents. Singing was thought to 'facilitate learning' and was described as 'a tool that allows children to access other parts of the curriculum, such as composing, instrument playing, PSHE, geography, fiction books and French.' Singing was thought to 'reinforce learning in other subjects', such as the report in one school that autistic pupils were more able to 'access parts of the curriculum through song' than by traditional means.

If you are a teacher, have you ever had any training in vocal health?

Overview

Two main areas of concern arise from the answers to this question; the first being that (i) teacher education courses have not (historically) provided a large amount of guidance regarding vocal health (if at all)[17] and that (ii) where respondent

---

[17] For a more detailed insight into the challenges to vocal health from teaching, see the new Sing Up web-based resource *Inside the Voice: The Sing Up Guide* by S. Barr and J. Williams (2011). This reviews data *inter alia* from over 3,000 voice clinic patients in a survey by the Voice Care Network (UK) in 2003. See also (1) Bassi, I., Assunçao, A., de Medeiros, A., de Menezes, L., Teixeira, L., & Cortes Gama, A. (2009). Quality of life, self-perceived dysphonia and diagnosed dysphonia through clinical tests in teachers. *Journal of Voice,* doi:10.1016/j.jvoice.2009.10.013; (2) Munier, C. &

teachers have received detailed guidance, this is a result of a Sing Up intervention or private singing lessons.

Detail

Those teachers, who do remember receiving guidance about vocal health, describe it in terms such as 'not much, [I] just picked it up along the years.' Others referred to the subject being covered very briefly, for example, 'it may have been mentioned in one lecture, sixteen years or so ago...', or 'not that I can remember – probably a few minutes in three years' and 'a little bit, but I do need a reminder as it was a while ago.' For teachers who were not music specialists, they described having 'four two hour sessions of Music in the three years' they spent training to be a primary teacher. This would seem to indicate that any coverage of the topic of vocal health (if at all) would have had to fit into this eight-hour general introduction to music teaching. Amongst the teachers who trained as music specialists, the reported picture was hardly improved, for example, 'even though I studied music, we had little training in vocal health and preparation to sing'.

By contrast, those teachers who felt more confident and competent regarding their vocal health cited two main areas of support and/or guidance. Some described how it was 'only through Sing Up training' that they had been introduced to the importance of some aspects of vocal health. Another teacher reported that it was 'only at a Sing Up conference' that vocal health had been introduced as a necessary topic. Others reported receiving private singing lessons that had helped them greatly. Sadly, some teachers had 'developed...vocal problems' and, as a result of working with speech therapists to address these issues, had 'received formal training in this area.'

Kinsella, R. (2008). The prevalence and impact of voice problems in primary school teachers. *Occupational Medicine*, 58(1): 74-76.; (3) Roy, N., Merrill, R. M., Thibeault, S., Parsa, R. A., Gray, S. D. & Smith, E. M. (2004). Prevalence of voice disorders in teachers and the general population. *Journal of Speech and Hearing Research*, 47 (2): 281-293.

Have you suffered illness and time from work due to poor vocal health or loss of voice?

Overview

Although the majority of responses were positive, there were a number of comments that indicated that poor vocal health is affecting teaching practitioners with particularly heavy rehearsal schedules. Some responses indicated that poor vocal health had become an expected part of their teaching lives. Both experienced and newly qualified teachers reported problems with their voices[18].

Detail

Of those respondents who reported problems with their voice, many reported that they 'often suffer with sore throats', suffer 'occasional' bouts of laryngitis, or that 'I have lost my voice…during my teaching career.' Some had experienced vocal weakness as a result of their work, stating that 'I do feel my voice is strained and sometime weaker depending on what I have done.' Others who experienced a regular loss of voice or poor vocal health were able to indicate the likely triggers, in many cases a combination of cold weather and increased work commitments. For example, 'I regularly lose my voice prior to Christmas productions and near the end of term', 'I regularly lose my voice each winter for a few days' and 'at busy times…my voice always feels a bit strained and overused.' One teacher described expecting to lose her voice '…normally two to three days a year when rehearsing heavily.'

Although few of the respondents reported taking time off school as a result of poor vocal health or loss of voice, many described continuing to work despite vocal problems. One teacher had 'not had time off, but [her] voice has suffered

---

[18] For an official perspective on the importance of vocal health for teachers, see:
http://www.teachernet.gov.uk/teachers/issue25/primary/features/Vocalsupport_Primary/

lately.' Despite having over twenty years experience in the classroom, she was concerned that her 'voice may be affected.'

Both newly qualified teachers and teachers who had recently taken on the responsibility for music provision within a school setting also reported problems with vocal health. One teacher described how 'this is the first year I have taught only music and at this stage in the school year – I feel as though my voice is struggling.' Some teachers had experienced significant bouts of vocal ill health, including one music specialist who had 'lost [her voice] for a week in May' and had not yet fully recovered, as well as a teacher who had had to take time off school, was prescribed medication, and 'had sessions with a speech therapist who taught me vocal exercises.'

Have you shared anything that you have learned in this Sing Up training scheme with your colleagues?

Overview

The vast majority of responses to this question provided a list of activities and information that teachers who had attended a Sing Up training scheme had later shared with their colleagues on return to the school. These included: (i) the creation of a favourites list, or CDs of favourite songs for offline access, (ii) teaching of songs to other staff members, (iii) guidance on classroom management issues during singing sessions, (iv) identification of cross-curricular and curriculum linked songs, (v) guidance regarding vocal health, (vi) leading singing workshops with teaching and/or support staff, (vii) an introduction to the Sing Up website and (viii) the creation of song sheets and distribution of the Sing Up magazine. Responses that indicated no sharing of information following the

Sing Up training were most likely to be made by members of staff who had (or felt they had) sole responsibility for singing within their school community.

Detail
(i) The creation of a favourites list, or CDs of favourite songs for offline access

Popular ways of sharing information as a result of Sing Up training included putting 'a range of songs on the favourites list to make access easy for everyone' or creating 'CD files of songs' to enable offline access.

(ii) Teaching of songs to other staff members

Often, teachers reported that they had 'shared new songs…activities [and] warm ups', as well as having used the songs 'learnt on courses [to teach] them in staff meetings', or having 'taught them songs, discussed the benefits of singing.' Some reported that staff meeting time had been dedicated to practising 'some of the songs.'

iii) Guidance on classroom management issues during singing sessions

Advice on how to organise singing in the classroom was highlighted by some teachers, stating that they had shared 'tips to make organisation of classroom activities easier to manage, effective ways to start activities…ensuring [the] involvement of all pupils.'

(iv) Identification of cross-curricular and curriculum linked songs

Some teachers had introduced a regular updating of suggested songs for colleagues, such as, for example, in one school where they 'frequently send suggestions to… teachers for songs they might sing with their class e.g. for a particular topic.' Making teachers aware of appropriate material for cross curricula and topic based work was also described in providing 'specific songs that I have found for teachers that relate to class topics.' Other staff had worked through particular songs with their colleagues that 'would support literacy and numeracy' within the classroom.

(v) Guidance regarding vocal health

Some staff reported that they had led 'staff meetings based on vocal health' as a result of their Sing Up training.

(vi) Singing workshops with teaching and/or support staff

Many schools reported workshops being held in order to allow time during the school day to share their Sing Up experiences with colleagues. 'Two staff meetings have been used to share the training. Ideas are passed on after each training session and warm ups shared in whole school singing sessions.' One teacher described how she 'ran a workshop for the staff… working through some of the songs' and another told how 'staff meeting sessions' were used 'to support teachers in their own classroom music.' Some schools reported 'inset training with support staff on playground songs' ensuring that the impact of the training was reaching a wide variety of staff within the school setting.

(vii) An introduction to the Sing Up website

Respondent who were teachers had taken time to introduce colleagues to the Sing Up website. 'I have made the rest of the staff aware of the Sing Up website' described one teacher. Some had formalised this introduction into a meeting such as 'I have run staff meetings based on…introducing the Sing Up website' and 'I have given a staff meeting where I have introduced the site.' Others had organised a 'workshop for the staff' introducing the website and encouraged all members of staff to sign into the website.

(viii) The creation of song sheets and distribution of the Sing Up magazine

For some respondents, it was important to create and distribute further materials related to the professional development that they themselves had received. These teachers 'provided written sheets and song packs for access' over and beyond the online access of the website. They were keen to 'pass on [the] magazine to [their] colleagues.'

By contrast, a very small number of responses indicated that little sharing of information had taken place, as the respondent had (or felt they had) sole responsibility for singing within their school community. In response to the questions asking if they had shared anything with their colleagues, some respondents replied 'no. I'm afraid they rely on me' or 'no, they leave all that kind of thing to me.'

What commitment have you made to continue developing your own singing and the singing of children?

Overview

The commitments made by respondent towards their own, and their children's singing can most easily be divided into three main areas: (i) the continuing professional development, (ii) a commitment to singing as a daily and central activity in school life and (iii) a commitment to the extended opportunities for participation in singing through (a) young singing leaders, (b) links with the community and (c) additional choirs and musical groups for pupils.

Detail

(i) The continuing professional development of teachers

Many responses described ways in which teachers and other participants wished to further their own understanding of, or expertise in, singing. For some, this was part of a personal developmental journey, related to the need to 'continue to develop [their] own repertoire, continue to perform and continue to do vocal exercises to maintain and improve [their] technique.' Some seemed to have discovered (or rediscovered) their own voices, stating that they wanted 'to continue singing myself and improving my own voice as I am enjoying singing so much now.' Others had recently 'joined a local choral society', planned to 'take singing lessons', or 'attend...a singing [and] conducting summer school.' Some expressed a desire to continue their commitment to singing through an academic route, 'studying...choral education at Masters level.'

For some respondents, the continuing commitment to singing was directed towards the support of others, for example, one teacher described the desire to 'keep encouraging and supporting non specialists with singing in their classrooms.' This aim was reflected in the comments of another respondent who wished to 'support...various members of staff develop their singing ability by asking them to lead warm ups and providing them with helpful and relevant resources.'

(ii) A commitment to singing as a daily and central activity in school life

Many responses to this question were given in relation to the centrality of singing in their school's life and the commitment to maintain this. Expressed simply, one teacher replied 'we sing at least one song EVERY day.' Another described the aim to 'continue to make good quality singing the core of the class music lessons and to provide opportunities for singing throughout the school day, not just in specialist music lessons.' For some, the established pattern of 'daily singing [was] to continue.' One teacher was more specific about when and how singing would take place, describing how the pupils would continue to sing 'together in different styles of songs for assemblies, both the whole school and through Key

Stage 1 and Key Stage 2', as well as 'developing sing[ing] through different festivals.' One teacher listed the singing activities that had been implemented within their school setting that now served as a framework for the school day, beginning with the 'schools breakfast club' and ending with the 'after school choir.'

(iii) A commitment to the extended opportunities for participation in singing through (a) young singing leaders

Many teachers described their ongoing commitment to the development and support of young singing leaders, stating that 'we will work to train up another group of young leaders each year.' Another respondent reported that a group of 'junior song leaders' had been established, 'to lead warm ups, class singing, school singing and community projects.'

iii) A commitment to the extended opportunities for participation in singing through (b) links with the community

Links with the community were to be strengthened through singing at a number of schools. Some, with the establishing of a 'parent choir', whilst others through the development of 'links with other schools' and pupils performing and contributing 'to community events.' In one school, children were being 'encouraged...to access the newly arranged community choir.'

iii) A commitment to the extended opportunities for participation in singing through (c) additional choirs and musical groups for pupils.

Many of the responses listed the variety of extra curricular clubs and choirs that had been established to allow pupils to sing. Pupil choirs have been established in many schools, for example, 'I run a school choir (Years 3, 4, 5 and 6 [pupils]) and a Year 5 and 6 choir for more advanced singing.' Teachers were 'provid[ing] regular performance opportunities within the school...to sing and perform to the school community.' Some schools had organised a 'recording of a CD...giving the Year 5 and 6 boys a track for themselves' in order to highlight an 'ongoing commitment to maintain[ing] a healthy balance of boys and girls in the school choir.' Schools had established a tradition of an 'end of year musical' with the desire of creating a 'reputation that the children know how to perform with confidence.'

Further comments

Overview
Given the opportunity to provide additional comments, the majority of responses were positive and demonstrated one of two main points: that of (i) the success of the Sing Up initiative and (ii) the usefulness of the Sing Up resources. Of those who took the opportunity to offer constructive criticism, the main areas of concern were (iii) the Sing Up website.

Detail
(i) The success of the Sing Up initiative

A selection of the comments made have been reproduced in full and require no further explanation.

'Who would have thought Sing Up could have generated so much in such a short space of time. Imagine if it was on top of government agendas in the future.'

'Please keep the funding for this superb resource – it would be a real shame to lose it.'

'I love Sing Up and so do my children at school.'

'Sing Up has been the most brilliant of initiatives. Even the parents are singing the songs when they drop their children off in the mornings and the children absolutely love singing. Thank you very much.'

'Congratulations to the staff who have delivered the courses. All [of the] organisation has been exemplary. A good government initiative.'

'It is impossible to explain what effect the Sing Up culture has had on our young people – it has been enormous in terms of confidence, enjoyment, musical engagement, understanding of how it fits in with various cultures and how it can be used as a positive tool across the curriculum.'

(ii) the usefulness of the Sing Up resources

Many teachers specifically praised the quality of resources provided through the Sing Up website and magazine. One stated that 'the resources are INVALUABLE and we use them regularly.' Some found that the resources were particularly helpful for non specialist teachers, stating that 'the Sing Up website is an extremely useful resource especially for staff who are unsure of singing...it's a good reminder of how different songs sound, for music and words.' Some found that sections of the website or magazine could easily be used to support learning objectives within the classroom setting, remarking that 'Sing Up is a brilliant resource. Easy to access and download all I need for a complete lesson. Great!' Another teacher explained how the Sing Up materials had become 'an absolutely invaluable resource' in their school.'

(iii) The Sing Up website

As the public interface between Sing Up and the many thousands of users, it is perhaps unsurprising that the website attracted some constructive criticism. Some teachers found the site to be 'very slow...doesn't always load and allow us to play songs.' Some acknowledged that the speed of site was restricted by hardware issues, stating that 'the website works very slowly on our school system (it works fine at home) so [I] struggle to play the backing tracks straight from the site.' A few teachers had been put off using the website in the classroom as they found it 'very difficult to access...putting you off using it.' Others described 'the computer site' as 'very frustrating as it frequently locks.' Requests for further training were made, as some teachers had received little or no guidance as to 'how to get the best use out of it. I have only recently discovered that if I log in I can just get a backing track.'

There was some debate concerning the differences between the old and new versions of the Sing Up website. Some felt the 'first website was brilliant because it was really easy and simple to navigate...the new website is really poor in terms of functionality. Quite often the page freezes and is extremely slow to navigate.'

By contrast, one respondent passed on 'congratulations to the researchers and technical advisers for the website.'

Conclusion

Over one thousand detailed responses were received from adult participants related to their experiences of Sing Up workforce development sessions. The overwhelming sense conveyed by their comments is positive, both at a personal level and also professionally. This includes evidence of a positive 'halo' effect, with reports of other colleagues, children and, in specific cases, whole school culture benefitting. In general, the comments suggest that there is now more and better quality singing in the respondents' schools and workplaces. The professional development experiences have led to improved knowledge about singing, as well as increased confidence in individual singing skills.

When this workforce development data is set alongside the latest analyses of Sing Up's impact on children across the country (related to the singing behaviour and development of approximately 10,000 children, as well as information on their attitudes to singing), there is a considerable body of evidence to suggest that singing has a more significant (and beneficial) place in many English schools.

It is to be hoped that the underlying features of the Sing Up programme will continue to be supported at national and local levels to ensure that singing becomes commonplace for all those who learn and teach in our schools – from nursery through to secondary levels, and not confined to those who have been fortunate enough to participate in the fixed-term current Primary-age initiative. Then the reported musical and other-than-musical benefits of music in general, and singing in particular (embracing physical, social and psychological – including emotional and cognitive benefits), will become routinely accessible and experienced by everyone.

Appendix I: List of reported qualifications in Music and/or Singing

4-year B.Ed Honours degree with Music as main subject. Grade 6+ piano.

6th form at Huddersfield Tech. College (now the University) doing instrumental and singing studies

A basic singing qualification obtained 1 day a week for a year.

A degree

A GCSE

A Level

A level Music

A level Music

A Level Music

A level music, B. Ed Hons in Music and Education, Grade 8 piano and oboe

A Level Music, Grade 4 Jazz piano and Grade 4 piano

A Level Music, Grade 8 piano

A Level Music, Grade 8 Piano. Grade 7 Clarinet, Grade 5 Saxophone, Grade 5 Singing

A Level Music, Grade 8 Piano, Several other lower grades on different instruments

A Level Music, Grade 8 violin

A Level Music, Trinity College of Music Grades I-VI violincello

A Level Music Violin Grade 7, Piano Grade5

A Level Music and ALCM pianoforte

A Level Music, B Mus (Hons) Music, PGCE Secondary Music

A Level Music, Grade 8 Flute

A Level Music, Grade 8 Flute.

A Level Music, Grade 8 piano and oboe.

ABRSM Grade 8 Piano ABRSM Grade 6 Saxophone, B.Ed (Hons.) Primary (Main subject Creative Arts/Music)

A.L.C.M. BEd (hons)- Music main subject

ABRSM Grade 8, B Ed (music specialist subject)

ABRSM Flute up to ADV Cert, ABRSM Violin up to Grade 5 ABRSM, Piano up to Grade 5 , ABRSM Theory up to Grade 5 BA(Hons) Music with Theatre Studies

ABRSM Grade 5

ABRSM Grade 5 Distinction , ABRSM Grade 5 Theory of Music

ABRSM Grade 5 Singing, ABRSM Grade 5 Theory of Music

ABRSM Grade 5 theory, Grade 8 clarinet , GCSE Music

ABRSM Grade 8, Thames Valley University Musical Theatre, Singing Gr 8

ABRSM Grade 8 in piano and flute, B.Ed Hons. in Music and Education

ABRSM Piano Grade 8, ABRSM Alto Saxophone Grade 7

ABRSM Violin, ABRSM Piano, GBSM Music PGCE Music

ABSM Violin teaching, ABSM Piano Teaching, GBSM Music, PGCE Music

ABRSM (violin teaching), ABRSM (piano teaching), PGCE (Music secondary)

AGSM (oboe) Author: 'A Reed Blown in the Wind' and 'Puffit's Oboe Pocket-Sized problem Solver'

ALCM

ALCM

ALCM B.Ed (Hons)

ALCM, LTCL Cert.Ed

ALCM for both violin and piano

ALCM in piano and singing Music Diploma - OU

ALCM, LTCL.CERT.ED

A Level, Singing Grade 7, Kodaly Certificate

A Level Music

A- level Music. Grade 5 piano, Grade 6 violin

A-level Music, Grade 7 Piano

Ancient piano and guitar exams (Grade 7 nearly 25 years ago, much unused!)

ARCM DipRCM Perfs

ARCM piano teacher and performer and Cert Ed as a secondary classroom teacher of music

ARCM, LGSM

ARCM

As Hungarian primary teacher I have to teach music and singing to children between 6-14 with Kodály method as it is part of the teacher degree. That means 4 year study: singing-solmization for primary school, methodology of music education, music literature.

AS Level

AS Level Music, various ABRSM instrumental grades

As part of my teaching diploma in senior primary work - specialism "Classroom Music"

Associate Board Grades to 5 for clarinet, also play guitar

Associate of the London College of Music, Teacher's Certificate with music main subject

Associate of the Victoria College of Music (piano)

Associated Board Grade 8 singing and Diploma in Music Education

Associated Board Piano grades 1-7. Music A level

Associateship of the London College of Music

ATCL, ALCM

AVCM Music, A Level Music (particularly song) formed part of my degree

BA (QTS) in music

BA (QTS) music was my main subject

B Ed Hons, Grade 8 voice and piano

BEd music

BEd, Grade 8 piano & Oboe

BMus (Hons) and DipABRSM in Singing Performance

BMus, Hon ALCM

BMus, Hon ALCM

BEd Hons - Music and Education, Grade 8 piano, Grade 8 oboe

BA Hons (Cantab) GRSM (Hons), LRAM (piano teaching), ARCM. (violin teaching)

BA in Music (Durham University) and MMus in Composition.

BA (Hons) Music, ALCM(piano/theory), PGCE (Primary music specialist)

BEd (Hons)

BEd (Hons) music main subject, ALCM in singing

BEd (music main subject), ABRSM Grade 8 piano and flute

BEd (music) Hons

BED Honours in Music and Education

BEd Hons in Music and Education.

BEd in Music and Education

BEd Music and Education, Grade 8 theory of music, Grade 7 piano

BEd in Music, Grade 8 Piano/Flute, Grade 6 Cello

BMus

BMus, ABRSM

BMus, ABSM (Piano Teaching Diploma), Currently studying for MA in Community Music, No formal qualification as a singer though!

BA (Ed) in Education and Music, LRSM in Music in the School Curriculum

BA (Hons)

BA (Hons)

BA (Hons)

BA (Hons) from Dartington College of Arts, inc. main studies in N. Indian Classical Singing and Community Arts

BA (Hons) in maths and music, ABRSM Grade 8 in piano and cornet.

BA (Hons) in music and a PGCE in music teaching

BA (Hons) in Music from Dartington College of Arts, I graduated in 1997

BA (Hons) in Music from Exeter University, 1990. PGCE specialising in Music from Exeter University.

BA (Hons) Music

BA (Hons) Music

BA (Hons) Music

BA (Hons) Music, University of Leeds PGCE

BA (Hons) Music & Theatre, Dartington College of Arts

BA (Hons) Music PGDip Music

BA (Hons) music and education studies, Piano Grade 8, Clarinet Grade 6

BA (Hons) Music and English

BA (Hons) Music and English, Grade 8 Piano, Grade 6 Piano, Grade 5 Flute

BA (Hons) Music with QTS

BA (Hons) Performing Arts, De Montfort University

BA (Hons), PGCE (Secondary Music)

BA (Hons), PGCE Grade 8 Piano and Violin

BA (Joint Hons) Music and Media Studies, music performance weighted. Piano 1st study, voice 2nd. Grade 8 singing.

BA Creative Arts (Music, Art and Drama). Grade 8 piano, theory and voice.

BA Degree (Ord) in Music and English

BA Fine Art/Music, LTCL (recorder). Cert. MusEd

BA Gen Hons (Bristol)., Diploma in Music Education.

BA Honours in Music

BA Honours Music , PGCE Secondary Music Specialist

BA Hons

BA Hons

BA Hons

BA Hons, LTCL, Estill Voice training system level 1 and 2, ABCD Intermediate choral conducting

BA Hons Postgraduate Certificate from London Institute of Ed. LLCM (Singing performance)

BA Hons (Music)

BA Hons and Grade 8 piano and theory

BA Hons, CASMAP music, York St John, A Level Music, GCSE Music, Grade 8 Flute, Grade 7 piano

BA Hons Music

BA Hons from Liverpool University, PGCE from Exeter University was a primary course with music as a specialism

BA Hons in Music

BA Hons in Music/Maths: double first class, MA in Music-Theatre (contemporary, avant-garde NOT musical Theatre), CPD Primary Music (Kodaly),

Intermediate Musicianship (distinction)

BA Hons in performance arts, Grade 8 voice, Grade 8 theory, Grade 7 flute.

BA Hons Music

BA Hons music

BA Hons Music

BA Hons Music

BA Hons Music ABRSM Diploma

BA Hons music CT ABRSM teaching certificate

BA Hons Music Grade 8 piano and clarinet, Working towards Grade 8 Voice

BA Hons Music, Grade 7 Singing, Grade 8 Piano

BA Hons Music, Grade 8 Singing

BA Hons Music, PGCE (Music specialism)

BA Hons Music, PGCE secondary music

BA Hons Music and Psychology

BA Hons Music and Psychology

BA Hons Music, PGCE in Music, Grade 8 Piano, Grade 8 Trumpet

BA Hons Music Nott.1977, PGCE London University Institute of Education 1978

BA Hons Music QTS, Advanced Certificate, Clarinet Grade 8 - Singing, Piano and Theory

BA Hons Music with Theatre Studies. ABRSM Grades 1- advanced certificate Flute, ABRSM Grade 5 piano, ABRSM Grade 5 violin.

BA Hons Performing Arts - Music

BA Hons Performing Arts, grade 8 piano

BA Hons QTS in Music and Education, MA in Community Music, and Grade 8 ABRSM in Singing.

BA Hons (QTS) Music

BA Hons, MMus.

BA in Music, A. Mus. A (Australia)

BA in Music from University of York, ABRSM Grade 8 singing

BA in Performing Arts

BA in Primary Education and Music.

BA Joint Honours in Music and History - majored in Voice. Grade 6 Plano

BA Music

BA (Hons) Music, ATCL

BA (Hons) Music, PGCE Secondary Music

BA Music Leeds, PGCE Music Reading, LRSM - Piano Teaching

BA Music major, PGCE (SA equivalent) in Music teaching method, Grade 6 singing

BA (Hons) Music, Grade 8 Piano and clarinet

BA Special Hons in Music ,Univ of Bristol, PGCE in Music Ed Univ of Reading

BA with elements of music

BA with Music Major from Rhodes University South Africa, ABRSM Grade 8 plus advanced certificate in performance in Flute, Grade 6 Piano, Grade 6 Voice, Grade 8 Recorder

BA (Hons) / PGCE

BA (Hons) in music, Grade 6 singing RAM

BA (Hons) Music, Music Diploma (violin teaching)

BA (Hons) Music, PGCE

BA (Hons) Music/Drama, PGCE Music/Phys Ed.

BA (Hons) teacher training and QTS with music education. ABRSM Grade 7 piano, ABRSM music theory, ABRSM grade 5 clarinet

BA (Hons)English and Music - University of Lancaster

BA (Hons)Music

BA, ALCM

BA. Hons Open. Dipolma music Open, Grade 8 violin Grade7 piano

BA; M.Mus; Certificate of Kodály Music Education (CKME), LRAM Piano teacher

Bachelor of Arts

Bachelor of Music (Hons), University of Manchester

Bachelor of Music Degree and various instrumental

exams through the ABRSM

Bachelor of Music Degree with Honours.

BA Ed Music

BA Hons ARCM performance cello Grade 8 singing Grade 7 piano

BA Hons Music

Bachelor of Music degree. GTP (Music and Music Technology)

BEd - music specialism, Grade 7 singing

BEd (music) 1976

BEd degree with music as main subject, Diploma in piano VCM

BEd Honours Degree Grades 1-8 in Piano and Flute playing

BEd Hons in Music

BEd in Music, MEd Creative Arts in Education, Grade 8 clarinet, Grade 6 piano

BEd in Music and Education, Grade 8 euphonium, Grade 7 piano, Grade 6 'cello

BEd Music

BEd specialising in music

BEd, Dip Mus Dartington, Grade 8 singing and piano

BMus

BMus, Advanced Certificate in Music and Movement for the Early Years (Dalcroze)

BMus music degree

BMus (2:1)

BMus (Hons)

BMus (Hons), Grade 8 singing, Grade 8 trumpet, Grades in Piano and Theory

BMus (Hons), MMus PG Diploma (oboe), Dalcroze Certificate

BMus (Hons) from Lancaster University, ALCM diploma on trumpet

BMus (Hons) Univ London

BMus (Hons), ATCL clarinet performance

BMus (Hons), City University, London, Grade 8 ABRSM (piano), PGCE Primary

BMus Birmingham Uni, PCS in workshop skills from GSMD

BMus, MTeach (Music specialty)

BMus Hons

BMus Hons, ARCM

BMus Hons, Grade 8 singing, LTCL (music education)

BMus Hons, Dip ABRSM (Performance)

BMus(Hons), GRNCM, No singing qualifications

BMus(Hons) Birmingham Conservatoire (1st study clarinet)

BMus, MA

BMus, PGCE

BMus Hons Bham 1985

BSc Hons degree in Music from the City University, London

BSc Hons Electronic Music, PGCE Music

BSc Hons in Music from City University and Grade 8 in singing, viola, and Grade 4 Piano from the ABRSM

BSc (Hons) degree in Music , Advanced Certificate (postgraduate study) in Performance & Communication Skills

but have passed piano exams up to grade 5 . Played clarinet at school and self taught recorder and guitar

Cert Ed (Music specialisation), LTCL MUS ED

Cert Ed, 1976

Cert. Higher Education

Cert.Mus.Ed (Trinity)

Certificate in Professional development in primary music [Leicester University] Associated Board piano 1-7

Certificate of Education [main subject Music]

Clarinet Royal Academy of Music, Grade 2 piano royal academy of music grade 4.

Clarinet /piano grades

Clarinet grade 5 Trumpet grade 2

Clarinet grade 6

Creative Arts BA (hons) : Music & Art PGCE Secondary Music Grade 8 piano Grade 7 flute

CT ABRSM

Degree Grade 8 (Voice) Grade 6 (Piano) Grade 7 (Violin)

Degree in Music. Grade 8 singing

Degree level in music - Oboe being main instrument

Dip Mus Ed RSAMD Dip Performance RSAMD Post Grad Dip Performance RNCM

Dip RCM (Singing) DipRCM (Singing teaching)

DIP. RCM (OBOE TEACHING), GRSM (HONS), PGCE SECONDARY MUSIC

DipABRSM

diploma for teaching many years ago

Diploma in Education- Music for Adolescents. Masters Degree-Choral Education (Graduating July 2010)

Diploma in music (Open University) Grade 8 recorder, Grade 7 piano and clarinet

Diploma in music performance from Salford College of Technology, Grade 8 Flute, Grade 8 Theory, Grade 7 Piano

Diploma in popular music, Diploma in song

Diploma in popular music performance

Final year of degree in music , A-level Grade exams in piano and violin

French Horn Grade 6 , Theory Grade 5, O level

GBSM ABSM PGCE

GBSM and LTCL

GCE Music ABRSM Piano Grades 1-8 Clarinet 3-6, violin 1-5, theory 1-6, CT ABRSM (certificate of teaching)

GCE music O Level, Grade 5 piano, Grade 4 guitar, OU unit in music

GCSE

GCSE - Music

GCSE & A Level, also degree in music

GCSE and A Level, Music Grades 1-6 Piano Grades 1-5 Music Theory Grades 5 and 8, Singing BA in Music Performance

GCSE in Music

GCSE Music

GCSE music

GCSE Music, A level Music ,Grade 7 Clarinet Grade 4 Keyboard

GCSE Music A Level Music BA Ed Music

GCSE music A Level music

BA Hons Educational studies with QTS and music

GCSE music, Grade 5 Trumpet

GCSE Music, Grade 6 Clarinet

GCSE Music , Grade A

GCSE Music & Associated Board Grade 5 Flute & Theory, Grade 3 Baritone!

GCSE music (A), A Level music (B) Grade 8 Flugel horn, Grade 6 piano ,

Grade 5 Theory, BA(QTS) with music degree 2:1

GCSE Music NEAB 1994 Grade C

GCSE O'level music Grade 5 piano

Grade 8 Clarinet

GLCM , LLCM Piano and Viola Teachers Certificate University of London

GMus

Grade & piano, Grade 4 violin & Grade 8 theory - also took music at 'O' level

Grade 2 Classical guitar!!

Grade 4 Associated Board piano

Grade 4 in piano, Grade 5 in theory.

Grade 4 piano

Grade 4 pianoforte

Grade 4 Singing, Grade 5 Piano, plus Grade 2 Theory

Grade 4 piano and years old Grade 5 theory and Grade 4 violin.

Grade 5 ABRSM Piano A level Music

Grade 5 Ass Board (many years ago!)

Grade 5 baritone (brass instrument) AS level music (c)

Grade 5 flute

Grade 5 music theory Grade 5 recorder Grade 1 piano Certificate of music in Kodaly methods, Level 1

Grade 5 Music Theory, Grade 7 Piano, Grade 8 Tuba

Grade 5 Piano

Grade 5 Piano

Grade 5 piano

Grade 5 Piano Currently doing a BSc (Hons) in Music Composition and Technology at the University of Hertfordshire

Grade 5 Piano, Grade 4 Clarinet

Grade 5 piano, Grade 5 clarinet, GCSE music grade B

Grade 5 piano & flute

Grade 5 Piano (does that count?!)

Grade 5 piano and theory

Grade 5 Piano and Theory of Music - Guildhall School of Music

Grade 5 pianoforte

Grade 5 Pianoforte practical and theory

Grade 5 theory, GCSE Music, Grade 6 piano, Grade 6 clarinet

Grade 5 theory, Grade 5 recorder Certificate of music in level 1 Kodaly training

Grade 5 theory, Grade 6 violin

Grade 6 ABRSM

Grade 6 clarinet, Grade 5 piano, Grade 5 music theory, GCSE music

Grade 6 clarinet.

Grade 6 Piano, 0 level music

- Grade 6 piano, Grade 4 violin
- Grade 6 Piano, Grade 5 Theory of Music, Grade 3 Singing
- Grade 6 piano, Grade 5 violin
- Grade 6 Piano 1985 "O" level Music 1984
- Grade 6 piano and Grade 6 clarinet
- Grade 6 singing only
- Grade 6 Theory
- Grade 6 theory and pianoforte- Guildhall school of music and drama
- Grade 6 violin
- Grade 7 Associated Board, Grade 6 Violin, Grade 5 Theory and Piano
- Grade 7 Piano
- Grade 7 piano
- Grade 7 piano
- Grade 7 piano
- Grade 7 piano
- Grade 7 piano, A-Level music
- Grade 7 piano, Grade 5 flute, Grade 5 music theory, GCSE music
- Grade 7 Piano, Grade 8 Flute, Grade 5 Theory, GCSE Music, A Level music, BA Hons CASMAP
- Grade 7 piano, O level music
- Grade 7 piano, Associated Board Grade 6 violin, Associated board
- Grade 7 piano, Grade 3 violin, A Level music, BEd with music main subject.
- Grade 7 singing (about to take Grade 8), Grade 8 Violin, Music O' Level
- Grade 7 theory & practice (piano)
- Grade 8 - does this count?
- Grade 8 Cello, Grade 5 Piano
- Grade 8 cello, Grade 6 guitar, Grade 5 piano Grade 1 cornet
- Grade 8 clarinet
- Grade 8 Clarinet, ABRSM Grade 5 Music Theory, GCSE Music
- Grade 8 clarinet, Grade 6 piano, BEd Hons (Music)
- Grade 8 distinction in singing, Music A Level , Music (and French) BA pending
- Grade 8 Flute, A Level Music
- Grade 8 flute, Grade 5 cello, Grade 3 piano
- Grade 8 Flute, Grade 5 Cello , Grade 2 Piano
- Grade 8 flute, Grade 5 piano, Grade 2 clarinet , B.Ed (hons) music
- Grade 8 flute , Music semi-specialism for BA(Ed) Hons
- Grade 8 flute (with distinction)
- Grade 8 in bassoon, Grade 6 in piano, A Level in music
- Grade 8 in Piano and Violin
- Grade 8 music exams. MA in Voice
- Grade 8 musical Theatre GuildHall
- Grade 8 on the bassoon and flute, Grade 5 theory and Grade 6 piano.
- Grade 8 piano
- Grade 8 piano
- Grade 8 piano
- Grade 8 piano 2:1 music degree
- Grade 8 piano , BA (Hons) in Learning and Teaching (also HLTA)
- Grade 8 Piano, Diploma in Musicianship
- Grade 8 Piano, Diploma in Musicianship, B.Ed (music)
- Grade 8 piano, Grade 6 flute, Diploma in Musicianship, B.Ed (music)
- Grade 8 piano, O Level music
- Grade 8 Piano Studied music at teacher training college
- Grade 8 piano and Cert Ed.
- Grade 8 piano and oboe. B.Ed Hons. in Music and Education
- Grade 8 piano practical and grade 8 music theory
- Grade 8 piano, clarinet and French Horn. Went to Birmingham School of Music.
- Grade 8 piano, clarinet and theory. Studying for BA in music.

Grade 8 Piano. ALCM Piano.

Grade 8 piano. Trained as a school music teacher 1973 to 1977. BEd(Hons)

Grade 8 singing, Grade 5 piano, Performing Arts Degree, KS2 CPD Trinity music programme

Grade 8 singing, A level music, BA (Hons) Creative Arts

Grade 8 Singing, Distinction, GCSE and A Level Music Pre degree, Classical soprano, Royal College of Music, BMus (Hons) RCM, MMus Royal Welsh College of Music

Grade 8 singing

Grade 8 violin, Grade 8 piano, BA (Hons) Music, PGCE 11-18 Music

Grade 8 Voice, Grade 8 Clarinet

Grade 8 voice (1990), BEd Hons Music and Education.

Grade 9 Recorder, Grades 5 for piano and trumpet. Music Educator Level 3 Diploma.

Grade 9 singing, BA and MA in music

Grade Five Piano

Grade 5 Clarinet

Grade 6 piano, Course from NVPN run by Frankie Armstrong.

Grade 6 Clarinet Grade 5 piano

Grade 6 piano

Grade 7 piano, Grade 8 voice m Post Graduate Diploma in Music Therapy

Grade 8 flute, Grade 6 piano

Grade 8 piano and cello, BSc (Hons) Music

Grade 8 clarinet, Grade7 piano, DipMus, PGCE (music)

Graded exams in piano

Grades 4 & 5 Violin, Grade 5 Theory of Music, A Level music

Grades 5 and 8 singing, Grades 1-5 Music theory, Grades 1-6 Piano, BA Music Performance

Grades 6, 7 and 8 in Voice, Diploma ATCl, in Vocal Performance, Trinity College London

Grade 8 – piano, Grade 7 – clarinet, Grade 6 - saxophone

Graduate Diploma in Music

Graduate Diploma in Music

Graduate of London College of Music Grade 8 Piano, Grade 8 Clarinet

GRNCM

GRSM (Hon), Royal Academy of Music LRAM

GRSM (Hons), Dip. RCM, ARCM, etc.

GRSM (Royal Academy of Music)

GTCL 1st Class Honours

GTCL FTCL LTCL, but no specific singing qualification.

GTCL, LTCL

Guildhall School of Music Piano Grade 5, Guildhall

School of Music Theory Grade 6

Have done Level 1 Music with the Open University, currently doing level 2 and next year level 3.

Have passed piano and violin exams

Have piano and clarinet exams - Grade 4 Clarinet and Grade 5 piano

Higher diploma from Trinity College of Music, London

HND Modern music & composition

Honours Degree in Music. Grade 8 Distinction Organ, Grade 5 theory of music. Singing first instrument in Degree

I achieved GCSE music grade B

I gained Level 4 in piano and music theory with the Royal Schools of Music

I have a BEd degree in Creative Arts. I studied creative music, dance drama and art

I have a BEd specialising in Music I have piano and clarinet grade 7 and 8 respectively.

I have Grade 7 piano

I have Grade 8 flute and can play the piano to about Grade 4 standard.

I have Grade 8 flute, and have specialised in music as part of my teaching degree.

I have Grades 2 and 4 in Flute.

I have Grade 8 combined percussion, a percussion

performance certificate, Grade 5 piano and Grade 5 theory.

I only went to Grade 6 in learning the piano.

I play flute and a very very tiny bit of piano. I have O level music!

If you mean Grade 5 piano and singing Music O Level (how far back is that!)

I'm not sure if it counts! I have a B.Ed. (Hons) with music as my specialist subject.

Just basics: AS Level Music Grade 5 singing

Just piano and clarinet exams

LAT for Voices Foundation

Level 2 Singing and will be doing level 3 Grade 8 in September.

Liverpool institute of performing arts diploma in song, access to music diploma in popular music

LRAM (oboe) GRSM 1st class hons

LRAM LGSM

LTCL

LTCL

LTCL piano teaching

LTCL (GMT), also B.Ed in Education and Music

LTCL diploma (instrumental)

LTCL Piano

LTCL, BMus (Hons), LRAM, ALCM

LTCL, GTCL

LTCM AVCM B.Hons music lead subject

MMus. BA Hons

MA (Cambridge University) in Music LGSM - piano performance

MA (Huddersfield), 1994; MPhil (Newcastle), 2003; LMusTCL, 1981.

MA (Music), MA (Mus Ed)

MA Community Music

MA in Composition of Music for Film/TV/Theatre. BA (Hons) Popular Music Studies , I started a PGCE in Music but did not complete it.

MA in Compositional Skills

MA Vocal/operatic Studies, Churchill Fellow 2005, PGCE, Estil, Kodaly, Advisory Teacher Status

Master in Music, RNCM, Post Graduate Diploma in Performance, RNCM Bachelors degree in Music with honours, RWCMD

Misc Assoc. Board exams in piano to Grade 8 & oboe to Grade 7 (all done while at school)

MMus

Music A Level, Grade 7 clarinet, Grade 4 Keyboard

Music A Level, Grade 8 piano, saxophone & clarinet

Music A Level

Music degree

Music degree

Music degree

Music degree (BA Hons)

Music Facilitation - OCNSEM Level 3 Grade 8 violin, Grade 5 theory

music facillitator in the community

Music 'O' Level, Grade 5 Theory, Grade 5 Piano

Music o'level (if that counts!)

Music theory Grade 5, clarinet Grade 8, piano Grade 5

My certificate in education (teaching qualification) was for education, French and music. I achieved Grade 7 singing many years ago!

My degree is Education and Music/ Various associated board qualifications.

N/A.

N/A

N/A - I am a project manager

O level in music. Grade 7 piano.

O' level music, Grade 4 pianoforte

O level Music, Grade 8 clarinet, Grade 6 piano, Grade 6 theory

O level music, Grade 8 trumpet

O level music (1975), Grade 7 theory of music (1976), Grade 3 piano (2010)

O Level music grade E, Grade 3 piano

O Level music, Grade 5 violin

O' Level, A' Level and B.Ed Hons in music Grades 3-8 flute with Associated Board Grades 1-6 piano Grade 2 clarinet Grade 6 theory

Only GCSE Music

Only Grade 5 voice and Grade 3 piano - but enough to give me a bit of confidence.

Only Grade 8 ABRSM

Only piano and recorder exams

Only to grade 5 Music - theory and playing

Open University diploma in music

PGCE, vocal artist 3 (Grade 6-8)

PGCE music, Grade 8 singing

PGCE Post 16, BTEC National Diploma in Popular Music, Degree in Pop Music Grade 5 and 8 Singing

Piano - Grade 5, Flute - Grade 4, Oboe -Grade 4

Piano - grade 6

Piano - grade 8

Piano (RSM) Grade 4

piano exams - taken a long time ago!

Piano Grade 8, Violin Grade 6, A Level music, Music main subject at college

Piano Grade 5

Piano Grade 5, Music Theory Grade 5

Piano Grade 6, O level music

Piano Grade 6 (theory Grade 5)

Piano Grade 7, Recorder Grade 5

Piano Grade 7, Viola Grade 4

Piano Grade 8

Piano Grade 8, oboe Grade 7

Piano Grade 8 (many years ago)

Piano Grade 8, ABRSM, violin Grade 6, Theory Grade 7

Piano Grades 1-5, music theory and Double Bass Grades 1-5.

Piano: Grade 5 Clarinet: Grade 8 Music Theory: Grade 5 Lifelong practitioner in all 3 areas (30+ years)

Pianoforte Grade 7.

Primary music specialism during my BEd Honours course, not a specific singing qualification.

RBSM Grade 8 piano RBSM Grade 7 flute BA (Hons) Creative Arts PGCE Secondary Music

Red Ribbon - Royal Church Chorister Grade 8 percussion Grade 2 Piano, Grade 2 Double Bass

Royal College of Music Theory Grades 1-7, Piano Grades 1-6

RSM Grade 5 Piano and Theory of Music

RSM Grade 5 pianoforte, RSCM Red medallion - chorister O level/CSE Music

RSM Grade 6 singing

RSM Grade V Piano Teaching Degree - Music 2nd subject

RSM Grade 7 piano. Main subject studied at college.

Screen Music, National Film and Television School OCN Level 2 Early Years Music Leader Qualification

Secondary school and Conservatory in Russia. Theory and history of music, lecturer, piano as second specialisation.

Singing Grade 8 (ABRSM), Music / Dance Hons Degree-Creative Arts, Music A Level, Music O Level, Music Theory Grade 5 (ABRSM)

Teacher of music (studied in Argentina)

Teaching Certificate in Junior Education, specialising in Music.

Theory Grade 5, Clarinet Grade 8 Piano Grade 5

Took grades on piano accordion and flute and self taught on organ and piano & guitar

Took music grades in piano up to Grade 3

Undergraduate Degree (BSc in Science and Music), Master of Arts in Music Performance

Up to Grade 4 (practical and theory) Piano. Music was my secondary subject at university.

Up to Grade 6 in piano forte and theory with the London College of Music

Up to Grade 6 piano. Music was part of my

Combined science degree.

various Royal College of Music exams

violin Grade 4,

violin Grade 6

Vocal Force participant

Appendix II: Respondents' qualifications in music and/or singing across the research strands

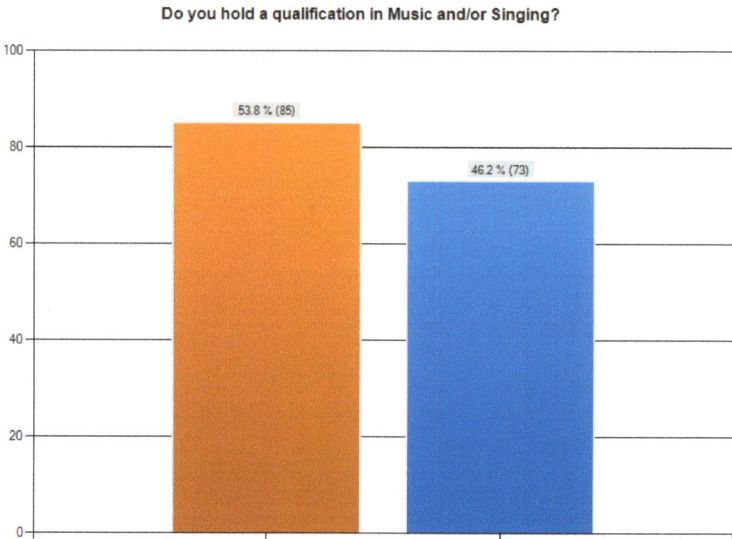

Figure 22: Respondents' qualifications in Music/Singing (SAGE 1)

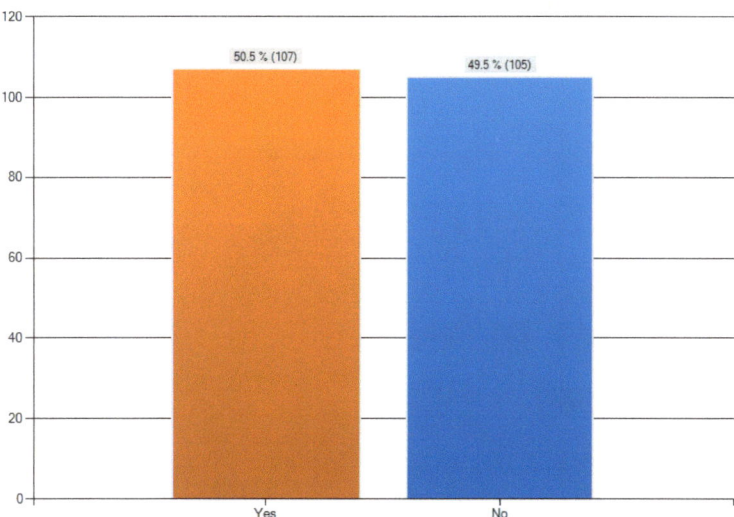

Figure 23: Respondents' qualifications in Music/Singing (SAGE 2)

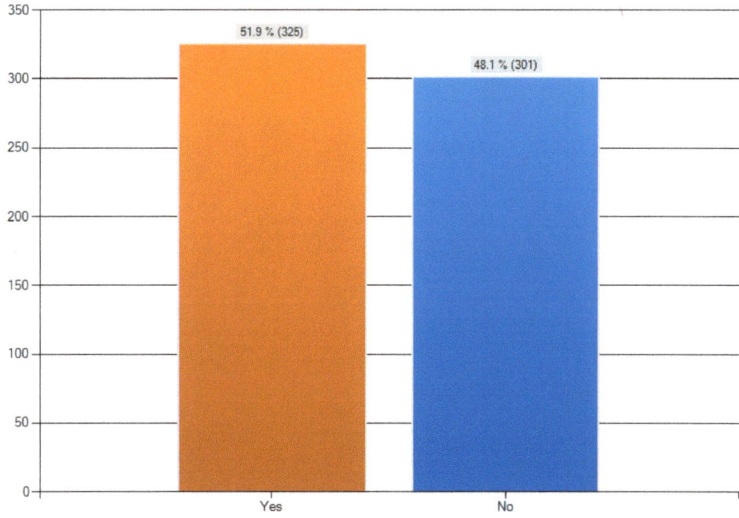

Figure 24: Respondents' qualifications in Music/Singing (SAGE 3)

Appendix III: QTS (strands)

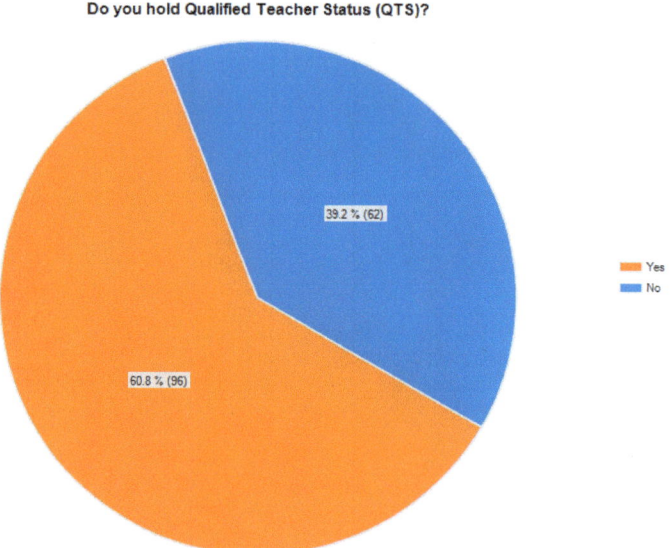

Figure 25: Do you hold Qualified Teacher Status? (SAGE 1)

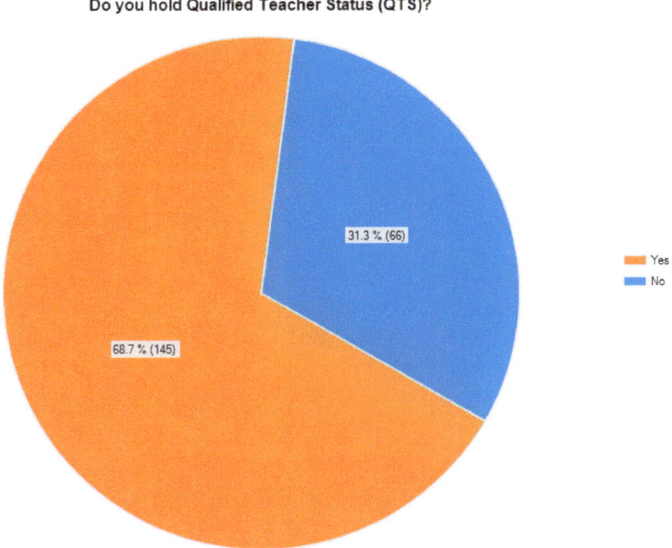

Figure 26: Do you hold Qualified Teacher Status? (SAGE 2)

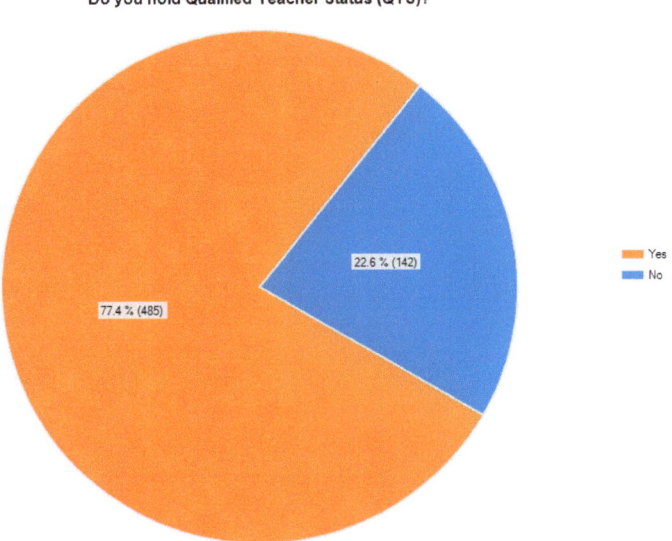

Figure 27: Do you hold Qualified Teacher Status? (SAGE 3)

Appendix IV: Masters in Teaching & Learning (other)

I already hold a Masters Degree from the OU

ABRSM CT Plus

Already have

Already have MA in Primary Ed.

Already started MA in Education in 2009

Am midway through my Foundation Degree in Early Years.

Am undertaking a Foundation degree in Teaching and Learning at present

BA (Hons) Applied education studies

but i have no formal music qualifications

completed masters in education

completing masters in teaching presently

CPD music course (Trinity Guildhall)

CT ABRSM

Currently working on CPD KS2 Trinity Guildhall/The Open University

Don't know what this is but possibly if it would help

GTP Primary as from Sept 2010

Have already achieved a Masters degree

Have completed Postgraduate Diploma in Inclusive Education. Plan to complete Masters within 2 years

Have MA in Theology would like more music qualifications

Have recently gained my masters in Ed (Visual Impairment)

I already have a MA in Primary Education (1998)

I am currently doing this in enabling learning (special needs).

I am just completing my MA Music (my Dissertation is in The Impact of the Legacy of the Folk Song Collectors on Music Education) and commence an MA in Education in October

I have already completed a Masters in Education

I have done various O.U. courses over the years.

I have investigated gaining QTS to recognise my Australian qualifications but have been told I am ineligible and would need to do a PGCE which I cannot consider.

I would consider the above if I had some financial support in place to be able to afford it.

I would like to achieve my QST Status

I've just completed a masters in education management

LEADING FROM THE MIDDLE

MA Creative and critical practice in education

MA Early Education

Masters in Primary Maths - Roehampton (or similar)

N/A - I am a project manager

NPQH

Performance Diploma with the ABRSM

Perhaps in Early Years - how children learn and impact of music on the way they learn

Post Graduate Certificate with EYPS

See above

SEN

SEN award for coordinators

Training as teacher of dyslexia

Appendix V: Groups normally lead

+ 20 KS2 pupils in choir - all year groups

Adults - training teachers

Adults from April 2009

Adults only when we get together to rehearse a special occasion song, e.g. a member of staff leaving or getting married

All class teachers teach music and singing. I support this work

All primary. Year 6 choir

All pupils have learning difficulties

All special needs children

All varying of special educational needs

all year in after school club

Also lead Yr1-4 when covering for Music Coordinator

also older people and people with learning disabilities

And 11 years experience of doing the same in secondary schools years 7-13

As a Kodály teacher the methodology is based around vocal work

Aside from yr5 6 I also plan to use at Summer School

assemblies - Main teaching Yr3

Assist in leading singing assemblies

At the moment I only sing with primary school children on an irregular basis.

Because we are an all-age special school with a high staff to pupil ratio, it is important that the adults receive as much encouragement as the students to engage in musical activities.

Can work with all age groups

Children have SEN, most have statements

choir - years 2-6

Choir throughout the school class year 1 and 2.

Church worship

currently but have worked with senior school students to 18 until recently

From this September I will just be working in Primary Schools

Hardly any now, in role as supply teacher

Has varied - is different each year

Have lead years 3-6 in past

Have ran KS 2 choir as well

Higher Education students - some mature

Hoping to start with Reception & Y1 soon

I also lead a music group outside school which includes a number of singers. This is made up of children from school year 5 to school year 13.

I am about to start maternity leave, so this question may be less relevant now.

I am not a school teacher

I am Secondary trained so I have also covered years 7-13

I currently work with these age groups in small groups of pupils with EBSD

I don't lead singing groups currently but use my singing skills to enhance instrumental tuition.

I don't teach or lead any singing

I don't teach singing, but I kind of give tips to the choirs that I lead

I have also directed an Upper Voice Youth Choir and worked with Y7 - Y13

I have led singing in KS1 and KS2.

I have recently branched out into old peoples' homes...

I help throughout KS1 and KS2 as required

I help with choir for Years 2 to 6 but am not lead teacher

I lead a community singing group consisting of children in KS2

I particularly enjoy working with adults who have little singing experience and work with them to produce a performance in a short space of time.

I teach singing on the wards to sick children across the age range and in the Primary classroom here at the hospital

I teach songs in Songs of Praise across all year groups. The choir is from Years 3 - 6.

I will be leading KS1 singing from September

I work in both areas but I don't lead.

I work in Children's Services in a non-teaching management role

I work with a community choir and organise community singing events throughout our cluster

I work with all ranges, but mostly adults

In role as vocal leader and teaching private lessons

In Soundmakers

In whole school singing

Includes training for adults

KS1 and KS2, SEN

Lead worship in my local church

Lev Krev projects

Limited use of singing and this is not taught as such

LUNCH TIMES!

Mostly adults

Mostly Y5/6 if not hymn practice for whole school

My choirs include some school age children.

My school is specialist ASD provision

My staff work with Year 4 upwards

N/A

N/A

N/A - I am a project manager

None

None

None

None

None but sing a little in piano lessons and lots with my own children

Not Teaching yet

Occasionally includes Key Stage 1 children

Older than Year11 sometimes, including adults

only as part of Primary languages Y3-6

plus adult group involving some teenagers

Plus whole school assemblies

Plus Years 7 - 13 at previous schools

Predominantly adults, but occasional work with children in all age groups

Pre-school, usually 9 months up to 4 yrs. 11 months

Pupils with SLD

Rarely opportunities in curriculum for secondary school

SEN in school and out of school, PRU

SEN school - throughout the school. I am a Year 1 teacher at present but have taught in Primary and Seniors.

Singing Assembly

Singing Club open to all (pre-school and adults included)

special needs

special needs school 3-19

staff choir

Teach strings wider opps. now

Teach the busking repertoire to the community choir I sing in.

The Saturday Singing classes are for below 16, so all ages will attend

The senior aged pupils are in a special school.

This is for the last 5 years. Previously 10 years up to Year 13

Used to do all this. Have now been squeezed out. Run a music assembly.

variable

varies

We are a cross phase choir

We are a special school and years mix more than usual

We are due to amalgamate in Sept 2010 when I shall be responsible for music delivery for Key Stage 2 as well.

we sometimes have the whole school or key stage singing together.

Weekly assembly to early years up to Y6

Weekly singing assembly

whole Primary range

Whole school singing, once a monthish

whole school/key stage groups

work in all Key Stages but not as vocal specialist

work in special schools aged 2 to 19 and with an adult choir with learning difficulties as acoompanist

Year 6 regulary as they are my class. The rest in whole school worship

Appendix VI: 'Other' formal responsibilities for music in school

A music specialist employed to teach class music/individual instrumental lessons.

Advanced Skills Teacher for teaching and learning including music and

performance

Advisory Teacher

also as a TA for other subjects

Also Head of the Arts

Am a peripatetic teacher with ArtForms - the music service in Leeds as well as being a governor

Am an HLTA and lead the music in the school.

and governor

and governor

and governor and music co-ordinator

AND teacher AND parent.

Another teacher is the Music Leader

Arts Coordinator

Arts Co-ordinator

As Deputy Director/Curriculum Advice, organising teaching and events

As headteacher

AST

AST

Class Teacher with responsibility for music

Community Education Worker for Media & Performance

Art

Co-ordinator

Co-ordinator

Co-ordinator

Co-ordinator

Creative team leader / AST music

Dedicated Music teacher to over 500 pupils at KS2

Deputy head/ Music subject leader

Development and delivery of Vocal Wider opportunities

do as an extra (there's no one on the staff)

Don't have a title as such - but Yr 5/6 music is my responsibility

Don't work in a specific school so no

Employed at school in various roles, including Clerk to Governors, as well as music

End of year 6 play and Medway concert plus

class knowing songs for Masses etc

For a day a week I am hired out by Tees Valley Music Service to schools to deliver short courses of whole class music curriculum to FS, KS1 & KS2.

Freelance Singing Leader

H O D Birmingham Music Service

Have been music co-ordinator at previous school

have responsibility for music and singing but not in schools -- see previous boxes

Have done in the past

Head of Music

Head Teacher

Head teacher so oversee all the curriculum

Headteacher

Headteacher

Headteacher

Headteacher

Higher Level Teaching Assistant

HLTA

HLTA (Higher Level Teaching Assistant)

Headteacher

I am a Higher Level Teaching Assistant with Music Co-ordinator as part of my responsibilities.

I am not a qualified teacher

I am not a school teacher. Occasionally schools hire my services

I am not a teacher

I am not teaching in primary school currently

I am not the Music coordinator in my school however I do work closely alongside the coordinator to plan and deliver assembly hymns/ whole school singing and co-lead performance club/ choir.

I don't have formal responsibility in the primary school I teach in, but use it a lot in what I do

I don't hold any formal responsibility, but all the music stuff is put in my pigeonhole!

I go into schools on a contract basis

I lead Music Centre and Summer School groups as well as teach groups of up to 4 and individuals

I'm not a teacher but I am responsible for the choir

I specialise in running choirs and orchestras and am entirely responsible for what I do with them. I also run an annual Big Sing for which I plan all the repertoire

I teach keyboards, violin and recorder

I teach music to KS 3 & 4, and play for assemblies

I teach recorder in another local school

I will be going forward for this.

I work in a community way with schools in the reach area and in the nursery. I also access groups of parents with very young children.

I work with the Music/ Arts co-ordinator to assist with the day to day running of Music in the school, especially music for assemblies and extra curricular groups

I'm a TA sometimes asked to lead singing activity but always with a teacher

I'm an HLTA but I am music co-ordinator in my school as we are a small school with more roles than teachers!

I'm not a teacher but can't get past this page without ticking one of the boxes

Lecturer in Voice.

Music and singing for shows.

Lev Krev

singer/project organiser/participant

Licensed Music Teacher

Literacy

music advisor

Music advisor as a freelancer or representing organisations and charities

Music co-ordinator

Music Consultant (Curriculum formation through KS2)

Music Coordinator

Music coordinator

Music Coordinator

Music coordinator

Music Co-ordinator

Music co-ordinator

Music Co-ordinator

Music co-ordinator

Music Co-ordinator

Music co-ordinator

Music co-ordinator

Music Co-ordinator and HLTA - teaching music throughout school

Music Co-ordinator for FS, KS1 and KS2

Music Co-ordinator for several years.

Music co-ordinator involving voluntary setting up and running of several choirs and clubs

Music co-ordinator Level 4 (HLTA) TA

Music curriculum support and enrichment from the Music Service.

Authority leader for area singing workshops and festivals

Music Instructor

Music leader

Music Leader

Music Leader and I teach Years 1-6 music

Music Manager

Music Specialist

Music specialist - two days a week

Music specialist teacher

Music Subject Leader

Music Teacher

Music teacher for primary years

Music tutor/school admin officer

N/A

N/A

N/A

N/A

N/A

N/A - County Music Service

N/A- I work for a music service

non-school based

Not a school teacher

not a school-based teacher

Not a teacher

Not a teacher

Not a teacher

Not a teacher

Not a teacher

Not a teacher

Not a teacher

Not a teacher

Not a teacher but member of the music team

Not a teacher, don't work in schools

Not applicable

Not as yet as am to start my NQT year in Sept

Not teacher

Now supply teacher but generally asked to take music lessons

Nursery Nurse

Nursery Nurse

Officially described now as an Instructor

Only in our special needs department !

Only just qualified - NQTs not allowed to take on extra responsibilities

Only within my own classroom

Our partner music services have some responsibilities in this area

Parent governor at one school; sessional music tutor

performing arts coordinator

Peripatetic staff

Peripatetic string and woodwind teaching

Peripatetic teacher working in several schools

Peripetetic and visiting community musician

PPA Supervisor / Music Coordinator

project manager working p/t for super sing up Cornwall from Dec09-March 2010

Ran a Vocalise programme to start choirs in the West Walton cluster which ended Dec 2009 currently following this up with further development paid for by the schools

Responsible for curriculum music

School Business Manager

School grounds

School pianist/accompanist

SENCO

shadow coordinator

shared music coordination

Share responsibility but not specifically music co-ordinator

Sing up co-ordinater

Singing and music coordinator

singing assembly , choir

Singing Support Leader for Derbyshire City & County Music Partnership

Specialist teacher visiting schools

Student teacher

subject co-ordinator

subject leader

Subject leader

Subject Leader

subject leader

Subject Leader for Music (inc CPD)

teach music

Teacher, Governor, Parent

Understanding the Arts coordinator (formally known as Music coordinator!)

Unpaid choir leader

unqualified teacher

Unqualified teacher I have a degree in social science & certificate in Education post 16

Until I gave up my permanent contract I was the music co-ordinator in my school

Visiting music teacher

Visiting Music Teacher

Visiting Music Teacher/Workshop Leader

visiting singing workshop leader

Visiting to deliver curriculum music, singing and, any Sing Up work which comes in.

Voluntary choir leader

was Music Coordinator and HLTA in a Lower school previous to working for Beds Music

weekly singing assemblies/special events

Wider opportunities practitioner

will hold a music coorindator role during first teching post

Work in 3 schools implementing music throughout the schools, but do teach history and sometimes swimming!

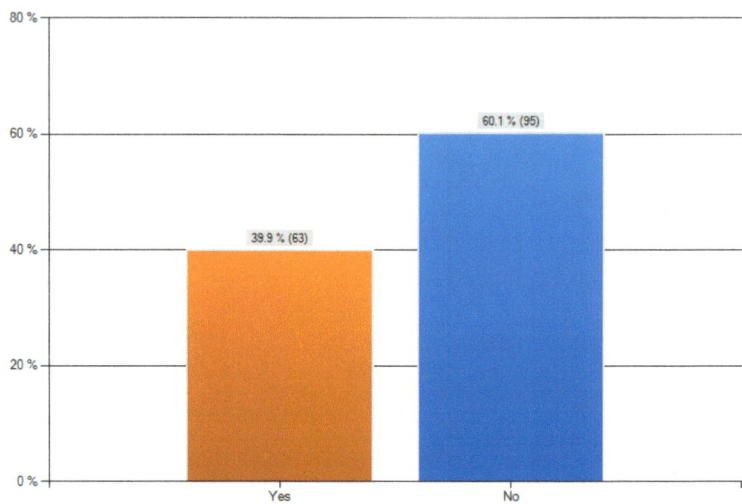

Figure 28: Respondents' formal responsibility for music at school (SAGE 1)

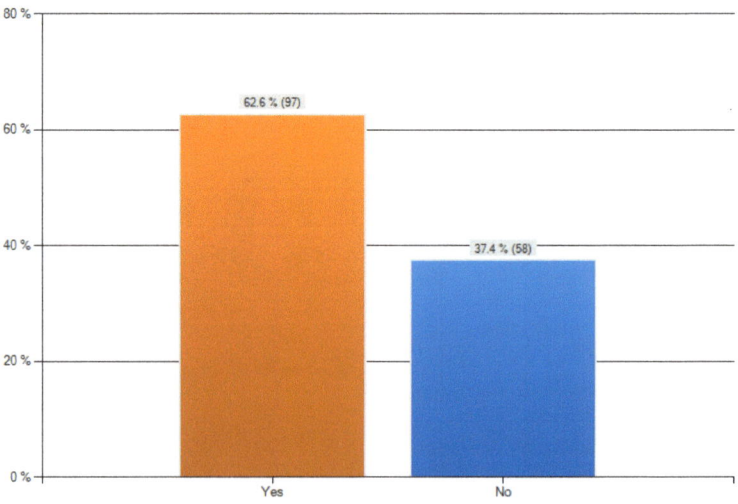

Figure 29: Respondents' formal responsibility for music at school (SAGE 2)

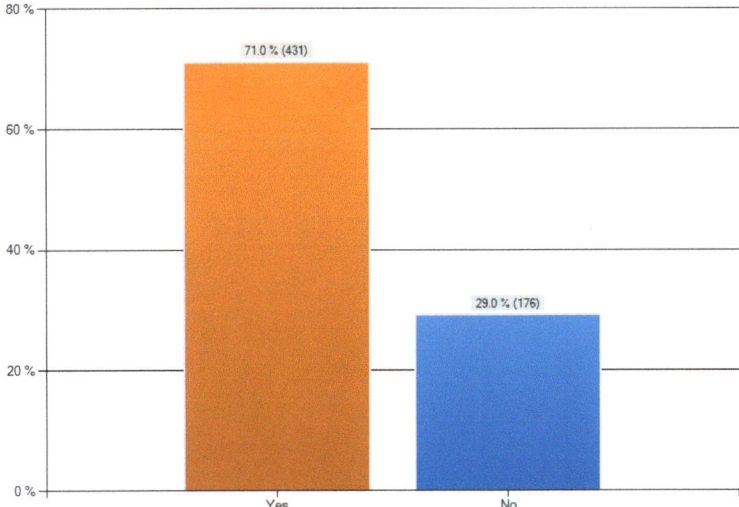

Figure 30: Respondents' formal responsibility for music at school (SAGE 3)

Appendix VII: Local authorities

Local authority	Number of responses	Percentage of total
Bristol City Council	38	4.09%
Stoke-on-Trent City Council	37	3.98%
North Yorkshire County Council	35	3.77%
Bradford City Council	27	2.91%
Cornwall County Council	26	2.80%
Kent County Council	26	2.80%
Kirklees Metropolitan Borough Council	25	2.69%
Hampshire County Council	25	2.69%
Suffolk County Council	24	2.58%
Cumbria County Council	24	2.58%
York City Council	23	2.48%
NOT APPLICABLE	20	2.15%
Cambridgeshire County Council	19	2.05%
Leicestershire County Council	18	1.94%
Norfolk County Council	17	1.83%
East Sussex County Council	17	1.83%
Hertfordshire County Council	17	1.83%
Derbyshire County Council	16	1.72%
Brighton and Hove City Council	16	1.72%
Durham County Council	15	1.61%
Devon County Council	15	1.61%
Birmingham City Council	15	1.61%
Lancashire County Council	14	1.51%
Cheshire County Council	14	1.51%
Lincolnshire County Council	13	1.40%
Trafford Metropolitan Borough Council	13	1.40%
Telford and Wrekin Borough Council	13	1.40%
Leeds City Council	12	1.29%

Local authority	Number of responses	Percentage of total
Nottingham City Council	11	1.18%
Hull City Council	11	1.18%
East Riding of Yorkshire Council	11	1.18%
Essex County Council	11	1.18%
Nottinghamshire County Council	10	1.08%
Sheffield City Council	10	1.08%
Northumberland County Council	9	0.97%
Manchester City Council	9	0.97%
South Gloucestershire District Council	8	0.86%
Bedfordshire County Council	8	0.86%
Dorset County Council	8	0.86%
Staffordshire County Council	7	0.75%
Somerset County Council	7	0.75%
Medway Borough Council	7	0.75%
Wirral Metropolitan Borough Council	6	0.65%
Stockport Metropolitan Borough Council	6	0.65%
Stockton-on-Tees Borough Council	6	0.65%
Sunderland City Council	6	0.65%
West Berkshire District Council	6	0.65%
Walsall Metropolitan Borough Council	6	0.65%
North Somerset District Council	6	0.65%
Buckinghamshire County Council	5	0.54%
Redcar and Cleveland Borough Council	5	0.54%
Leicester City Council	5	0.54%
Wiltshire County Council	5	0.54%
Oldham Metropolitan Borough Council	5	0.54%
Newham London Borough Council	5	0.54%
Wakefield City Council	5	0.54%
Gloucestershire County Council	5	0.54%
Yorkshire and the Humber	4	0.43%
Derby City Council	4	0.43%
Portsmouth City Council	4	0.43%
North East Lincolnshire Borough Council	4	0.43%

Local authority	Number of responses	Percentage of total
Oxfordshire County Council	4	0.43%
Warrington Borough Council	4	0.43%
Worcestershire County Council	4	0.43%
Middlesbrough Borough Council	4	0.43%
Salford City Council	4	0.43%
Halton Borough Council	3	0.32%
Tameside Metropolitan Borough Council	3	0.32%
Gateshead Metropolitan Borough Council	3	0.32%
Lewisham London Borough Council	3	0.32%
Calderdale Metropolitan Borough Council	3	0.32%
St Helens Metropolitan Borough Council	3	0.32%
Sutton London Borough Council	3	0.32%
Southampton City Council	3	0.32%
Bolton Metropolitan Borough Council	3	0.32%
West Sussex County Council	3	0.32%
Rotherham Metropolitan Borough Council	3	0.32%
Bury Metropolitan Borough Council	2	0.22%
Southwark London Borough Council	2	0.22%
Lambeth London Borough Council	2	0.22%
Wigan Metropolitan Borough Council	2	0.22%
Swindon Borough Council	2	0.22%
Ealing London Borough Council	2	0.22%
Waltham Forest London Borough Council	2	0.22%
Richmond upon Thames London Borough Council	2	0.22%
Knowsley Metropolitan Borough Council	2	0.22%
Slough Borough Council	2	0.22%
Merton London Borough Council	2	0.22%
Doncaster Metropolitan Borough Council	2	0.22%
Sefton Metropolitan Borough Council	2	0.22%
Redbridge London Borough Council	2	0.22%
Torbay Borough Council	2	0.22%
Shropshire County Council	2	0.22%

Local authority	Number of responses	Percentage of total
Surrey County Council	2	0.22%
Hounslow London Borough Council	2	0.22%
Bournemouth Borough Council	2	0.22%
Darlington Borough Council	2	0.22%
Luton Borough Council	2	0.22%
Plymouth City Council	2	0.22%
Rochdale Metropolitan Borough Council	2	0.22%
North Lincolnshire Borough Council	2	0.22%
Liverpool City Council	1	0.11%
Reading Borough Council	1	0.11%
Brent London Borough Council	1	0.11%
Southend-on-Sea Borough Council	1	0.11%
Poole Borough Council	1	0.11%
Peterborough City Council	1	0.11%
Windsor and Maidenhead Borough Council	1	0.11%
Wokingham District Council	1	0.11%
Bracknell Forest Borough Council	1	0.11%
Isle of Wight Council	1	0.11%
Warwickshire County Council	1	0.11%
Rutland County Council District Council	1	0.11%
Dudley Metropolitan Borough Council	1	0.11%
South Tyneside Metropolitan Borough Council	1	0.11%
Greenwich London Borough Council	1	0.11%
Hillingdon London Borough Council	1	0.11%
Thurrock Borough Council	1	0.11%
Croydon London Borough Council	1	0.11%
North West	1	0.11%
Coventry City Council	1	0.11%
North Tyneside Metropolitan Borough Council	1	0.11%
Wandsworth London Borough Council	1	0.11%
Blackburn with Darwen Borough Council	1	0.11%
Harrow London Borough Council	1	0.11%
Bexley London Borough Council	1	0.11%

Local authority	Number of responses	Percentage of total
Camden London Borough Council	1	0.11%
Bath and North East Somerset District Council	1	0.11%
Haringey London Borough Council	1	0.11%
Tower Hamlets London Borough Council	1	0.11%
Grand Total	929	100.00%

Appendix VIII: Local Authority representation across research strands

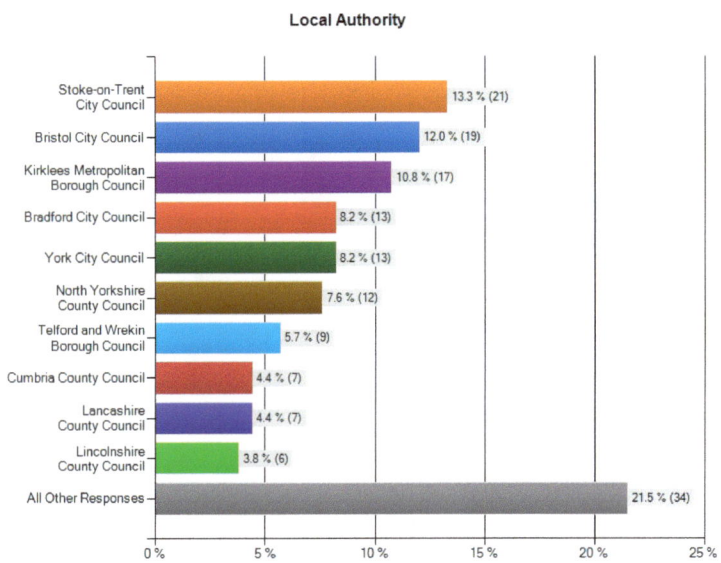

Figure 31: Local Authority representation (SAGE 1)

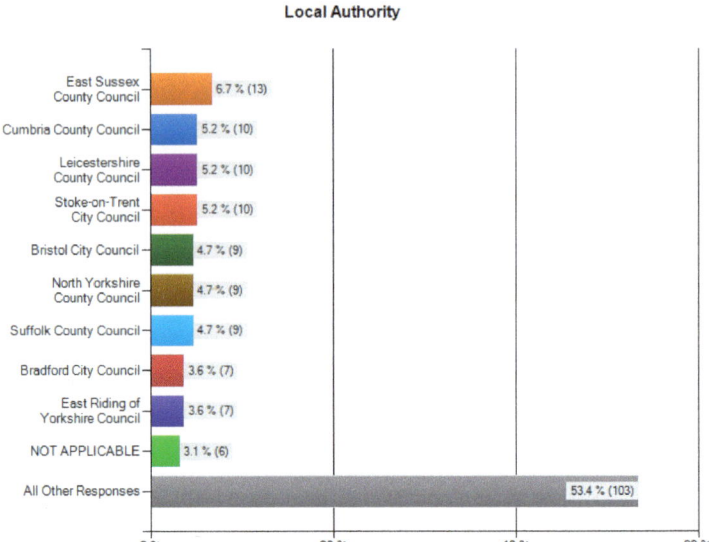

Figure 32: Local Authority representation (SAGE 2)

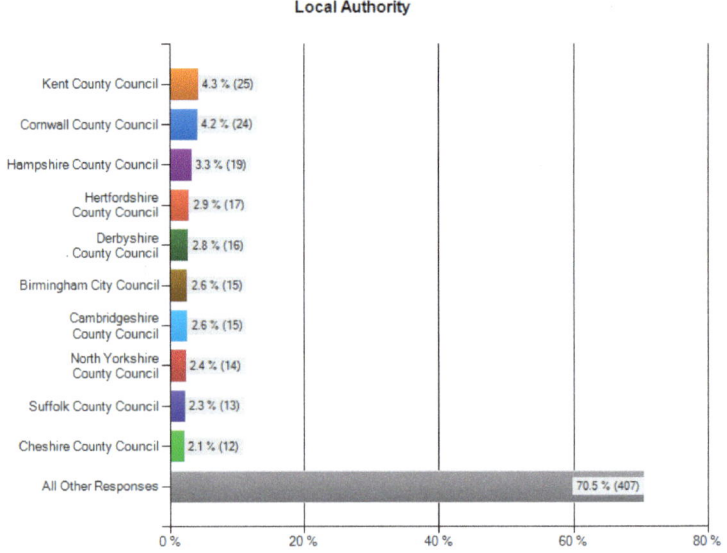

Figure 33: Local Authority representation (SAGE 3)

Appendix IX: Self efficacy, sex

Descriptives

	Respondents' sex			Statistic	Std. Error
Singing self efficacy	Prefer not to say	Mean		5.167421	.2861551
		95% Confidence Interval for Mean	Lower Bound	4.543942	
			Upper Bound	5.790899	
		5% Trimmed Mean		5.156611	
		Median		5.529412	
		Variance		1.065	
		Std. Deviation		1.0317470	
		Minimum		3.9412	
		Maximum		6.5882	
		Range		2.6471	
		Interquartile Range		1.9706	
		Skewness		.022	.616
		Kurtosis		-1.998	1.191
	Female	Mean		5.401401	.0327069
		95% Confidence Interval for Mean	Lower Bound	5.337204	
			Upper Bound	5.465597	
		5% Trimmed Mean		5.450825	
		Median		5.529412	
		Variance		.899	
		Std. Deviation		.9479353	
		Minimum		1.5882	
		Maximum		7.0000	
		Range		5.4118	
		Interquartile Range		1.2941	
		Skewness		-.737	.084
		Kurtosis		.542	.169
	Male	Mean		5.434683	.0921213
		95% Confidence Interval for Mean	Lower Bound	5.251208	
			Upper Bound	5.618158	
		5% Trimmed Mean		5.460233	
		Median		5.588235	
		Variance		.653	
		Std. Deviation		.8083607	
		Minimum		3.5294	
		Maximum		6.8824	
		Range		3.3529	
		Interquartile Range		1.1471	
		Skewness		-.608	.274
		Kurtosis		-.515	.541

Appendix X: Self efficacy, QTS

Descriptives

	Do you hold Qualified Teacher Status (QTS)?			Statistic	Std. Error
Singing self efficacy	Did not say	Mean		5.712418	.2985684
		95% Confidence Interval for Mean	Lower Bound	5.023918	
			Upper Bound	6.400918	
		5% Trimmed Mean		5.745824	
		Median		5.941176	
		Variance		.802	
		Std. Deviation		.8957051	
		Minimum		4.2353	
		Maximum		6.5882	
		Range		2.3529	
		Interquartile Range		1.5000	
		Skewness		-1.122	.717
		Kurtosis		-.162	1.400
	No	Mean		5.406080	.0631443
		95% Confidence Interval for Mean	Lower Bound	5.281684	
			Upper Bound	5.530476	
		5% Trimmed Mean		5.447905	
		Median		5.588235	
		Variance		.949	
		Std. Deviation		.9741432	
		Minimum		2.7059	
		Maximum		7.0000	
		Range		4.2941	
		Interquartile Range		1.4118	
		Skewness		-.525	.158
		Kurtosis		-.354	.314
	Yes	Mean		5.394970	.0354360
		95% Confidence Interval for Mean	Lower Bound	5.325393	
			Upper Bound	5.464547	
		5% Trimmed Mean		5.443253	
		Median		5.529412	
		Variance		.858	
		Std. Deviation		.9260946	
		Minimum		1.5882	
		Maximum		7.0000	
		Range		5.4118	
		Interquartile Range		1.2353	
		Skewness		-.801	.094
		Kurtosis		.826	.187

Appendix XI: Self efficacy, number of Sing Up training activities

Descriptives

	Number of Sing Up training activities attended			Statistic	Std. Error
Singing self efficacy	N/A	Mean		5.271579	.0502247
		95% Confidence Interval for Mean	Lower Bound	5.172815	
			Upper Bound	5.370344	
		5% Trimmed Mean		5.313335	
		Median		5.411765	
		Variance		.928	
		Std. Deviation		.9634769	
		Minimum		1.5882	
		Maximum		6.9412	
		Range		5.3529	
		Interquartile Range		1.3529	
		Skewness		-.596	.127
		Kurtosis		.086	.254
	1 session	Mean		5.347234	.0819780
		95% Confidence Interval for Mean	Lower Bound	5.185085	
			Upper Bound	5.509384	
		5% Trimmed Mean		5.392206	
		Median		5.529412	
		Variance		.901	
		Std. Deviation		.9489635	
		Minimum		2.0588	
		Maximum		6.9412	
		Range		4.8824	
		Interquartile Range		1.2941	
		Skewness		-.708	.209
		Kurtosis		.518	.416
	2 or 3 sessions	Mean		5.447467	.0693087
		95% Confidence Interval for Mean	Lower Bound	5.310662	
			Upper Bound	5.584272	
		5% Trimmed Mean		5.486909	
		Median		5.529412	
		Variance		.831	
		Std. Deviation		.9116132	
		Minimum		2.7059	
		Maximum		7.0000	
		Range		4.2941	
		Interquartile Range		1.2353	
		Skewness		-.627	.185
		Kurtosis		.004	.367
	3+ sessions	Mean		5.584083	.0553289

95% Confidence Interval for Mean	Lower Bound	5.475121		
	Upper Bound	5.693045		
5% Trimmed Mean		5.634435		
Median		5.705882		
Variance		.781		
Std. Deviation		.8835312		
Minimum		1.5882		
Maximum		7.0000		
Range		5.4118		
Interquartile Range		1.1765		
Skewness		-1.012	.153	
Kurtosis		1.882	.304	

Appendix XII: Knowledge of learners, sex

Descriptives

	Respondents' sex			Statistic	Std. Error
Knowledge of Learners	Prefer not to say	Mean		5.345238	.3182057
		95% Confidence Interval for Mean	Lower Bound	4.644872	
			Upper Bound	6.045604	
		5% Trimmed Mean		5.359788	
		Median		5.500000	
		Variance		1.215	
		Std. Deviation		1.1022970	
		Minimum		3.4286	
		Maximum		7.0000	
		Range		3.5714	
		Interquartile Range		1.7500	
		Skewness		-.343	.637
		Kurtosis		-.781	1.232
	Female	Mean		4.882850	.0389717
		95% Confidence Interval for Mean	Lower Bound	4.806355	
			Upper Bound	4.959345	
		5% Trimmed Mean		4.916456	
		Median		4.928571	
		Variance		1.258	
		Std. Deviation		1.1214107	
		Minimum		1.2857	
		Maximum		7.0000	
		Range		5.7143	
		Interquartile Range		1.5714	
		Skewness		-.396	.085
		Kurtosis		.007	.170
	Male	Mean		5.085343	.1186167
		95% Confidence Interval for Mean	Lower Bound	4.849098	
			Upper Bound	5.321589	
		5% Trimmed Mean		5.134818	
		Median		5.142857	
		Variance		1.083	
		Std. Deviation		1.0408570	
		Minimum		1.8571	
		Maximum		7.0000	
		Range		5.1429	
		Interquartile Range		1.5714	
		Skewness		-.647	.274
		Kurtosis		.308	.541

Appendix XIII: Knowledge of learners, QTS

Descriptives

	Do you hold Qualified Teacher Status (QTS)?			Statistic	Std. Error
Knowledge of Learners	Did not say	Mean		5.587302	.3135674
		95% Confidence Interval for Mean	Lower Bound	4.864214	
			Upper Bound	6.310389	
		5% Trimmed Mean		5.604938	
		Median		5.714286	
		Variance		.885	
		Std. Deviation		.9407022	
		Minimum		3.8571	
		Maximum		7.0000	
		Range		3.1429	
		Interquartile Range		1.2857	
		Skewness		-.443	.717
		Kurtosis		.143	1.400
	No	Mean		4.857753	.0783426
		95% Confidence Interval for Mean	Lower Bound	4.703403	
			Upper Bound	5.012104	
		5% Trimmed Mean		4.898114	
		Median		4.857143	
		Variance		1.436	
		Std. Deviation		1.1984120	
		Minimum		1.2857	
		Maximum		7.0000	
		Range		5.7143	
		Interquartile Range		1.7500	
		Skewness		-.412	.159
		Kurtosis		-.112	.317
	Yes	Mean		4.913523	.0418506
		95% Confidence Interval for Mean	Lower Bound	4.831349	
			Upper Bound	4.995696	
		5% Trimmed Mean		4.945386	
		Median		5.000000	
		Variance		1.180	
		Std. Deviation		1.0865036	
		Minimum		1.5714	
		Maximum		7.0000	
		Range		5.4286	
		Interquartile Range		1.4286	
		Skewness		-.405	.094
		Kurtosis		.039	.188

Appendix XIV: Knowledge of learners, number of Sing Up training activities

Descriptives

	Number of Sing Up training activities attended			Statistic	Std. Error
Knowledge of Learners	N/A	Mean		4.718995	.0600251
		95% Confidence Interval for Mean	Lower Bound	4.600955	
			Upper Bound	4.837036	
		5% Trimmed Mean		4.754143	
		Median		4.857143	
		Variance		1.311	
		Std. Deviation		1.1452063	
		Minimum		1.2857	
		Maximum		7.0000	
		Range		5.7143	
		Interquartile Range		1.5714	
		Skewness		-.440	.128
		Kurtosis		-.004	.255
	1 session	Mean		4.750831	.0961158
		95% Confidence Interval for Mean	Lower Bound	4.560649	
			Upper Bound	4.941012	
		5% Trimmed Mean		4.772118	
		Median		4.857143	
		Variance		1.192	
		Std. Deviation		1.0916659	
		Minimum		1.7143	
		Maximum		7.0000	
		Range		5.2857	
		Interquartile Range		1.5714	
		Skewness		-.276	.213
		Kurtosis		-.356	.423
	2 or 3 sessions	Mean		4.985050	.0823360
		95% Confidence Interval for Mean	Lower Bound	4.822524	
			Upper Bound	5.147576	
		5% Trimmed Mean		5.008121	
		Median		5.000000	
		Variance		1.166	
		Std. Deviation		1.0798260	
		Minimum		1.5714	
		Maximum		7.0000	
		Range		5.4286	
		Interquartile Range		1.5000	
		Skewness		-.225	.185
		Kurtosis		.128	.368
	3+ sessions	Mean		5.201247	.0658241

95% Confidence Interval for Mean	Lower Bound		5.071609	
	Upper Bound		5.330885	
5% Trimmed Mean			5.242756	
Median			5.285714	
Variance			1.092	
Std. Deviation			1.0449255	
Minimum			1.5714	
Maximum			7.0000	
Range			5.4286	
Interquartile Range			1.5714	
Skewness			-.534	.153
Kurtosis			.166	.306

Appendix XV: ANOVA - Knowledge of learners, number of Sing Up training activities

One-way Analysis of Variance (ANOVA)

ANOVA
Knowledge of Learners

	Sum of Squares	df	Mean Square	F	Sig.
Between Groups	38.877	3	12.959	10.736	.000
Within Groups	1102.065	913	1.207		
Total	1140.942	916			

Post Hoc Tests

Multiple Comparisons
Knowledge of Learners
Tukey HSD

(I) Number of Sing Up training activities attended		(J) Number of Sing Up training activities attended		Mean Difference (I-J)	Std. Error	Sig.	95% Confidence Interval	
							Lower Bound	Upper Bound
dimension2	N/A	dimension3	1 session	-.0318353	.1125761	.992	-.321580	.257910
			2 or 3 sessions	-.2660545*	.1016566	.045	-.527695	-.004414
			3+ sessions	-.4822519*	.0900342	.000	-.713979	-.250525
	1 session	dimension3	N/A	.0318353	.1125761	.992	-.257910	.321580
			2 or 3 sessions	-.2342193	.1279653	.260	-.563572	.095134
			3+ sessions	-.4504166*	.1189421	.001	-.756546	-.144287

2 or 3 sessions	dimension3	N/A	.2660545*	.1016566	.045	.004414	.527695
		1 session	.2342193	.1279653	.260	-.095134	.563572
		3+ sessions	-.2161973	.1086642	.193	-.495874	.063479
3+ sessions	dimension3	N/A	.4822519*	.0900342	.000	.250525	.713979
		1 session	.4504166*	.1189421	.001	.144287	.756546
		2 or 3 sessions	.2161973	.1086642	.193	-.063479	.495874

*. The mean difference is significant at the 0.05 level.

Appendix XVI: Knowledge of singing pedagogy, sex

Descriptives

	Respondents' sex			Statistic	Std. Error
Knowledge of Singing Pedagogy	Prefer not to say	Mean		2.042208	.4774984
		95% Confidence Interval for Mean	Lower Bound	1.062462	
			Upper Bound	3.021954	
		5% Trimmed Mean		1.896104	
		Median		.000000	
		Variance		6.384	
		Std. Deviation		2.5266843	
		Minimum		.0000	
		Maximum		6.8182	
		Range		6.8182	
		Interquartile Range		4.4318	
		Skewness		.610	.441
		Kurtosis		-1.349	.858
	Female	Mean		4.159334	.0654424
		95% Confidence Interval for Mean	Lower Bound	4.030903	
			Upper Bound	4.287766	
		5% Trimmed Mean		4.243495	
		Median		4.636364	
		Variance		4.000	
		Std. Deviation		2.0000130	
		Minimum		.0000	
		Maximum		7.0000	
		Range		7.0000	
		Interquartile Range		2.0000	
		Skewness		-1.022	.080
		Kurtosis		.061	.160
	Male	Mean		4.607143	.2000055
		95% Confidence Interval for Mean	Lower Bound	4.209340	
			Upper Bound	5.004946	
		5% Trimmed Mean		4.746032	
		Median		5.000000	
		Variance		3.360	
		Std. Deviation		1.8330803	
		Minimum		.0000	
		Maximum		7.0000	
		Range		7.0000	
		Interquartile Range		1.7045	
		Skewness		-1.577	.263
		Kurtosis		1.820	.520

Appendix XVII: Knowledge of singing pedagogy, QTS

Descriptives

	Do you hold Qualified Teacher Status (QTS)?			Statistic	Std. Error
Knowledge of Singing Pedagogy	Did not say	Mean		.899814	.3021196
		95% Confidence Interval for Mean	Lower Bound	.292362	
			Upper Bound	1.507267	
		5% Trimmed Mean		.635745	
		Median		.000000	
		Variance		4.473	
		Std. Deviation		2.1148371	
		Minimum		.0000	
		Maximum		6.8182	
		Range		6.8182	
		Interquartile Range		.0000	
		Skewness		2.059	.340
		Kurtosis		2.543	.668
	No	Mean		3.952189	.1303698
		95% Confidence Interval for Mean	Lower Bound	3.695514	
			Upper Bound	4.208864	
		5% Trimmed Mean		4.011036	
		Median		4.545455	
		Variance		4.589	
		Std. Deviation		2.1421948	
		Minimum		.0000	
		Maximum		7.0000	
		Range		7.0000	
		Interquartile Range		2.3182	
		Skewness		-.829	.148
		Kurtosis		-.485	.295
	Yes	Mean		4.426160	.0659065
		95% Confidence Interval for Mean	Lower Bound	4.296770	
			Upper Bound	4.555550	
		5% Trimmed Mean		4.541120	
		Median		4.727273	
		Variance		3.158	
		Std. Deviation		1.7770329	
		Minimum		.0000	
		Maximum		7.0000	
		Range		7.0000	
		Interquartile Range		1.7273	
		Skewness		-1.263	.091
		Kurtosis		1.098	.181

Appendix XVIII: Knowledge of singing pedagogy, number of Sing Up training activities

Descriptives

	Number of Sing Up training activities attended			Statistic	Std. Error
Knowledge of Singing Pedagogy	N/A	Mean		3.675440	.1044071
		95% Confidence Interval for Mean	Lower Bound	3.470252	
			Upper Bound	3.880629	
		5% Trimmed Mean		3.714765	
		Median		4.363636	
		Variance		4.894	
		Std. Deviation		2.2123475	
		Minimum		.0000	
		Maximum		7.0000	
		Range		7.0000	
		Interquartile Range		2.8182	
		Skewness		-.677	.115
		Kurtosis		-.909	.230
	1 session	Mean		3.886995	.1670737
		95% Confidence Interval for Mean	Lower Bound	3.556742	
			Upper Bound	4.217248	
		5% Trimmed Mean		3.942761	
		Median		4.363636	
		Variance		4.020	
		Std. Deviation		2.0048847	
		Minimum		.0000	
		Maximum		7.0000	
		Range		7.0000	
		Interquartile Range		2.0455	
		Skewness		-.875	.202
		Kurtosis		-.209	.401
	2 or 3 sessions	Mean		4.476051	.1331890
		95% Confidence Interval for Mean	Lower Bound	4.213286	
			Upper Bound	4.738815	
		5% Trimmed Mean		4.597643	
		Median		4.909091	
		Variance		3.300	
		Std. Deviation		1.8164561	
		Minimum		.0000	
		Maximum		7.0000	
		Range		7.0000	
		Interquartile Range		1.4545	
		Skewness		-1.326	.178
		Kurtosis		1.187	.355
	3+ sessions	Mean		4.818182	.0990902

95% Confidence Interval for Mean	Lower Bound	4.623081	
	Upper Bound	5.013283	
5% Trimmed Mean		4.969205	
Median		5.000000	
Variance		2.622	
Std. Deviation		1.6191469	
Minimum		.0000	
Maximum		7.0000	
Range		7.0000	
Interquartile Range		1.5455	
Skewness		-1.554	.149
Kurtosis		2.635	.297

Appendix XIX: ANOVA - Knowledge of singing pedagogy, number of Sing Up training activities

One-way Analysis of Variance (ANOVA)

ANOVA
Knowledge of Singing Pedagogy

	Sum of Squares	df	Mean Square	F	Sig.
Between Groups	249.923	3	83.308	21.301	.000
Within Groups	4075.290	1042	3.911		
Total	4325.214	1045			

Post Hoc Tests

Multiple Comparisons
Knowledge of Singing Pedagogy
Tukey HSD

(I) Number of Sing Up training activities attended	(J) Number of Sing Up training activities attended	Mean Difference (I-J)	Std. Error	Sig.	95% Confidence Interval Lower Bound	95% Confidence Interval Upper Bound
N/A	1 session	-.2115546	.1893949	.679	-.698902	.275793
	2 or 3 sessions	-.8006105*	.1724458	.000	-1.244345	-.356876
	3+ sessions	-1.1427414*	.1528351	.000	-1.536014	-.749469
1 session	N/A	.2115546	.1893949	.679	-.275793	.698902
	2 or 3 sessions	-.5890559*	.2195152	.037	-1.153908	-.024203
	3+ sessions	-.9311869*	.2044699	.000	-1.457325	-.405049
2 or 3 sessions	N/A	.8006105*	.1724458	.000	.356876	1.244345
	1 session	.5890559*	.2195152	.037	.024203	1.153908
	3+ sessions	-.3421310	.1888785	.268	-.828150	.143888
3+ sessions	N/A	1.1427414*	.1528351	.000	.749469	1.536014
	1 session	.9311869*	.2044699	.000	.405049	1.457325
	2 or 3 sessions	.3421310	.1888785	.268	-.143888	.828150

*. The mean difference is significant at the 0.05 level.

Appendix XX: Knowledge of musics, sex

Descriptives

	Respondents' sex			Statistic	Std. Error
Knowledge of Musics	Prefer not to say	Mean		4.94792	.382643
		95% Confidence Interval for Mean	Lower Bound	4.10573	
			Upper Bound	5.79011	
		5% Trimmed Mean		4.97685	
		Median		5.12500	
		Variance		1.757	
		Std. Deviation		1.325513	
		Minimum		2.500	
		Maximum		6.875	
		Range		4.375	
		Interquartile Range		2.062	
		Skewness		-.291	.637
		Kurtosis		-.499	1.232
	Female	Mean		5.03904	.044049
		95% Confidence Interval for Mean	Lower Bound	4.95258	
			Upper Bound	5.12551	
		5% Trimmed Mean		5.09705	
		Median		5.25000	
		Variance		1.541	
		Std. Deviation		1.241209	
		Minimum		1.000	
		Maximum		7.000	
		Range		6.000	
		Interquartile Range		1.750	
		Skewness		-.633	.087
		Kurtosis		.036	.173
	Male	Mean		5.43833	.108204
		95% Confidence Interval for Mean	Lower Bound	5.22273	
			Upper Bound	5.65394	
		5% Trimmed Mean		5.47731	

Median	5.62500	
Variance	.878	
Std. Deviation	.937077	
Minimum	1.500	
Maximum	7.000	
Range	5.500	
Interquartile Range	1.250	
Skewness	-1.074	.277
Kurtosis	2.901	.548

Appendix XXI: Knowledge of musics, QTS

Descriptives

	Do you hold Qualified Teacher Status (QTS)?			Statistic	Std. Error
Knowledge of Musics	Did not say	Mean		5.40625	.487426
		95% Confidence Interval for Mean	Lower Bound	4.25367	
			Upper Bound	6.55883	
		5% Trimmed Mean		5.43056	
		Median		5.50000	
		Variance		1.901	
		Std. Deviation		1.378648	
		Minimum		3.500	
		Maximum		6.875	
		Range		3.375	
		Interquartile Range		2.844	
		Skewness		-.346	.752
		Kurtosis		-1.608	1.481
	No	Mean		5.10445	.082986
		95% Confidence Interval for Mean	Lower Bound	4.94089	
			Upper Bound	5.26801	
		5% Trimmed Mean		5.16984	
		Median		5.37500	
		Variance		1.508	
		Std. Deviation		1.228078	
		Minimum		1.500	
		Maximum		7.000	
		Range		5.500	
		Interquartile Range		1.750	
		Skewness		-.679	.164
		Kurtosis		.006	.327
	Yes	Mean		5.05677	.047751
		95% Confidence Interval for Mean	Lower Bound	4.96300	
			Upper Bound	5.15053	
		5% Trimmed Mean		5.11464	
		Median		5.25000	

Variance	1.491	
Std. Deviation	1.221146	
Minimum	1.000	
Maximum	7.000	
Range	6.000	
Interquartile Range	1.625	
Skewness	-.679	.096
Kurtosis	.220	.191

Appendix XXII: Knowledge of musics, number of Sing Up training activities

Descriptives

	Number of Sing Up training activities attended			Statistic	Std. Error
Knowledge of Musics	N/A	Mean		4.88256	.066444
		95% Confidence Interval for Mean	Lower Bound	4.75188	
			Upper Bound	5.01325	
		5% Trimmed Mean		4.94014	
		Median		5.00000	
		Variance		1.532	
		Std. Deviation		1.237724	
		Minimum		1.000	
		Maximum		7.000	
		Range		6.000	
		Interquartile Range		1.500	
		Skewness		-.642	.131
		Kurtosis		.151	.261
	1 session	Mean		4.87707	.118103
		95% Confidence Interval for Mean	Lower Bound	4.64323	
			Upper Bound	5.11090	
		5% Trimmed Mean		4.93388	
		Median		5.00000	
		Variance		1.688	
		Std. Deviation		1.299137	
		Minimum		1.375	
		Maximum		7.000	
		Range		5.625	
		Interquartile Range		1.875	
		Skewness		-.607	.220
		Kurtosis		-.183	.437
	2 or 3 sessions	Mean		5.17273	.093576
		95% Confidence Interval for Mean	Lower Bound	4.98796	
			Upper Bound	5.35750	

	5% Trimmed Mean		5.23001	
	Median		5.37500	
	Variance		1.445	
	Std. Deviation		1.202011	
	Minimum		1.000	
	Maximum		7.000	
	Range		6.000	
	Interquartile Range		1.625	
	Skewness		-.660	.189
	Kurtosis		.104	.376
3+ sessions	Mean		5.36442	.070868
	95% Confidence Interval for Mean	Lower Bound	5.22483	
		Upper Bound	5.50400	
	5% Trimmed Mean		5.41846	
	Median		5.50000	
	Variance		1.246	
	Std. Deviation		1.116030	
	Minimum		1.000	
	Maximum		7.000	
	Range		6.000	
	Interquartile Range		1.500	
	Skewness		-.714	.155
	Kurtosis		.287	.308

Appendix XXIII: ANOVA - Knowledge of musics, number of Sing Up training activities

One-way Analysis of Variance (ANOVA)

ANOVA
Knowledge of Musics

	Sum of Squares	df	Mean Square	F	Sig.
Between Groups	39.930	3	13.310	9.140	.000
Within Groups	1277.185	877	1.456		
Total	1317.115	880			

Post Hoc Tests

Multiple Comparisons
Knowledge of Musics
Tukey HSD

(I) Number of Sing Up training activities attended	(J) Number of Sing Up training activities attended	Mean Difference (I-J)	Std. Error	Sig.	95% Confidence Interval	
					Lower Bound	Upper Bound
N/A	1 session	.005499	.127407	1.000	-.32244	.33344
	2 or 3 sessions	-.290162	.114118	.054	-.58390	.00357
	3+ sessions	-.481850*	.100345	.000	-.74013	-.22357
1 session	N/A	-.005499	.127407	1.000	-.33344	.32244
	2 or 3 sessions	-.295661	.144436	.172	-.66743	.07611
	3+ sessions	-.487349*	.133820	.002	-.83180	-.14290
2 or 3 sessions	N/A	.290162	.114118	.054	-.00357	.58390
	1 session	.295661	.144436	.172	-.07611	.66743
	3+ sessions	-.191688	.121237	.390	-.50375	.12037
3+ sessions	N/A	.481850*	.100345	.000	.22357	.74013
	1 session	.487349*	.133820	.002	.14290	.83180
	2 or 3 sessions	.191688	.121237	.390	-.12037	.50375

*. The mean difference is significant at the 0.05 level.

Appendix XXIV: The pupils in my group/class, sex

Descriptives

	Respondents' sex			Statistic	Std. Error
The Pupils in My Group/Class	Prefer not to say	Mean		5.526316	.3023454
		95% Confidence Interval for Mean	Lower Bound	4.860858	
			Upper Bound	6.191774	
		5% Trimmed Mean		5.558480	
		Median		5.763158	
		Variance		1.097	
		Std. Deviation		1.0473552	
		Minimum		3.7368	
		Maximum		6.7368	
		Range		3.0000	
		Interquartile Range		2.0132	
		Skewness		-.715	.637
		Kurtosis		-.801	1.232
	Female	Mean		5.517892	.0331275
		95% Confidence Interval for Mean	Lower Bound	5.452862	
			Upper Bound	5.582922	
		5% Trimmed Mean		5.575765	
		Median		5.684211	
		Variance		.857	
		Std. Deviation		.9257946	
		Minimum		1.0000	
		Maximum		7.0000	
		Range		6.0000	
		Interquartile Range		1.1579	
		Skewness		-1.152	.087
		Kurtosis		2.448	.175
	Male	Mean		5.527027	.0952995
		95% Confidence Interval for Mean	Lower Bound	5.337095	
			Upper Bound	5.716959	
		5% Trimmed Mean		5.554370	

Median	5.578947	
Variance	.672	
Std. Deviation	.8197970	
Minimum	3.5263	
Maximum	6.8421	
Range	3.3158	
Interquartile Range	1.1842	
Skewness	-.442	.279
Kurtosis	-.306	.552

Appendix XXV: The pupils in my group/class, QTS

Descriptives

	Do you hold Qualified Teacher Status (QTS)?			Statistic	Std. Error
The Pupils in My Group/Class	Did not say	Mean		5.868421	.3340580
		95% Confidence Interval for Mean	Lower Bound	5.078499	
			Upper Bound	6.658343	
		5% Trimmed Mean		5.944444	
		Median		6.263158	
		Variance		.893	
		Std. Deviation		.9448588	
		Minimum		3.7368	
		Maximum		6.6316	
		Range		2.8947	
		Interquartile Range		.9079	
		Skewness		-1.989	.752
		Kurtosis		4.252	1.481
	No	Mean		5.385213	.0668466
		95% Confidence Interval for Mean	Lower Bound	5.253433	
			Upper Bound	5.516993	
		5% Trimmed Mean		5.445280	
		Median		5.473684	
		Variance		.938	
		Std. Deviation		.9686987	
		Minimum		1.0000	
		Maximum		7.0000	
		Range		6.0000	
		Interquartile Range		1.1316	
		Skewness		-1.230	.168
		Kurtosis		3.275	.334
	Yes	Mean		5.557700	.0352172
		95% Confidence Interval for Mean	Lower Bound	5.488546	
			Upper Bound	5.626854	
		5% Trimmed Mean		5.610670	
		Median		5.736842	

Variance	.805	
Std. Deviation	.8971755	
Minimum	1.3684	
Maximum	7.0000	
Range	5.6316	
Interquartile Range	1.1842	
Skewness	-1.039	.096
Kurtosis	1.791	.192

Appendix XXVI: The pupils in my group/class, number of Sing Up training activities

Descriptives

	Number of Sing Up training activities attended			Statistic	Std. Error
The Pupils in My Group/Class	N/A	Mean		5.325359	.0521126
		95% Confidence Interval for Mean	Lower Bound	5.222855	
			Upper Bound	5.427863	
		5% Trimmed Mean		5.371379	
		Median		5.368421	
		Variance		.926	
		Std. Deviation		.9623206	
		Minimum		1.0000	
		Maximum		7.0000	
		Range		6.0000	
		Interquartile Range		1.1842	
		Skewness		-.911	.132
		Kurtosis		1.811	.263
	1 session	Mean		5.637823	.0936557
		95% Confidence Interval for Mean	Lower Bound	5.452343	
			Upper Bound	5.823304	
		5% Trimmed Mean		5.738874	
		Median		5.842105	
		Variance		1.035	
		Std. Deviation		1.0173616	
		Minimum		1.0000	
		Maximum		7.0000	
		Range		6.0000	
		Interquartile Range		.9474	
		Skewness		-1.802	.223
		Kurtosis		4.579	.442
	2 or 3 sessions	Mean		5.619810	.0632528
		95% Confidence Interval for Mean	Lower Bound	5.494892	
			Upper Bound	5.744728	

	5% Trimmed Mean		5.661164	
	Median		5.789474	
	Variance		.644	
	Std. Deviation		.8025879	
	Minimum		2.0526	
	Maximum		7.0000	
	Range		4.9474	
	Interquartile Range		1.1053	
	Skewness		-.925	.191
	Kurtosis		1.520	.380
3+ sessions	Mean		5.663115	.0528051
	95% Confidence Interval for Mean	Lower Bound	5.559107	
		Upper Bound	5.767123	
	5% Trimmed Mean		5.712586	
	Median		5.789474	
	Variance		.689	
	Std. Deviation		.8298973	
	Minimum		1.8421	
	Maximum		7.0000	
	Range		5.1579	
	Interquartile Range		1.0526	
	Skewness		-.946	.155
	Kurtosis		1.487	.309

Appendix XXVII: My teaching/singing leadership, sex

Descriptives

	Respondents' sex			Statistic	Std. Error
My teaching/singing leadership	Prefer not to say	Mean		5.763636	.3749601
		95% Confidence Interval for Mean	Lower Bound	4.928173	
			Upper Bound	6.599099	
		5% Trimmed Mean		5.826263	
		Median		5.600000	
		Variance		1.547	
		Std. Deviation		1.2436018	
		Minimum		3.4000	
		Maximum		7.0000	
		Range		3.6000	
		Interquartile Range		2.2000	
		Skewness		-.548	.661
		Kurtosis		-.807	1.279
	Female	Mean		5.683029	.0399218
		95% Confidence Interval for Mean	Lower Bound	5.604660	
			Upper Bound	5.761398	
		5% Trimmed Mean		5.779547	
		Median		5.900000	
		Variance		1.221	
		Std. Deviation		1.1049025	
		Minimum		1.3000	
		Maximum		7.0000	
		Range		5.7000	
		Interquartile Range		1.4000	
		Skewness		-1.216	.088
		Kurtosis		1.611	.176
	Male	Mean		5.859155	.1095184
		95% Confidence Interval for Mean	Lower Bound	5.640727	

	Upper Bound	6.077582	
5% Trimmed Mean		5.900626	
Median		6.000000	
Variance		.852	
Std. Deviation		.9228183	
Minimum		3.9000	
Maximum		7.0000	
Range		3.1000	
Interquartile Range		1.4000	
Skewness		-.616	.285
Kurtosis		-.594	.563

Appendix XXVIII: My teaching/singing leadership, QTS

Descriptives

	Do you hold Qualified Teacher Status (QTS)?			Statistic	Std. Error
My teaching/singing leadership	Did not say	Mean		5.825000	.3544362
		95% Confidence Interval for Mean	Lower Bound	4.986892	
			Upper Bound	6.663108	
		5% Trimmed Mean		5.833333	
		Median		5.750000	
		Variance		1.005	
		Std. Deviation		1.0024969	
		Minimum		4.6000	
		Maximum		6.9000	
		Range		2.3000	
		Interquartile Range		2.0500	
		Skewness		-.044	.752
		Kurtosis		-2.258	1.481
	No	Mean		5.572683	.0776827
		95% Confidence Interval for Mean	Lower Bound	5.419519	
			Upper Bound	5.725847	
		5% Trimmed Mean		5.658266	
		Median		5.700000	
		Variance		1.237	
		Std. Deviation		1.1122469	
		Minimum		1.7000	
		Maximum		7.0000	
		Range		5.3000	
		Interquartile Range		1.4500	
		Skewness		-1.017	.170
		Kurtosis		.989	.338
	Yes	Mean		5.737953	.0430839
		95% Confidence Interval for Mean	Lower Bound	5.653348	

	Upper Bound	5.822557	
5% Trimmed Mean		5.833377	
Median		6.000000	
Variance		1.179	
Std. Deviation		1.0856792	
Minimum		1.3000	
Maximum		7.0000	
Range		5.7000	
Interquartile Range		1.5000	
Skewness		-1.258	.097
Kurtosis		1.814	.194

Appendix XXIX: My teaching/singing leadership, number of Sing Up training activities

Descriptives

	Number of Sing Up training activities attended			Statistic	Std. Error
My teaching/singing leadership	N/A	Mean		5.537168	.0627860
		95% Confidence Interval for Mean	Lower Bound	5.413668	
			Upper Bound	5.660669	
		5% Trimmed Mean		5.629367	
		Median		5.800000	
		Variance		1.336	
		Std. Deviation		1.1560129	
		Minimum		1.4000	
		Maximum		7.0000	
		Range		5.6000	
		Interquartile Range		1.6000	
		Skewness		-1.080	.132
		Kurtosis		1.148	.264
	1 session	Mean		5.753043	.1015090
		95% Confidence Interval for Mean	Lower Bound	5.551955	
			Upper Bound	5.954132	
		5% Trimmed Mean		5.846860	
		Median		6.000000	
		Variance		1.185	
		Std. Deviation		1.0885627	
		Minimum		2.1000	
		Maximum		7.0000	
		Range		4.9000	
		Interquartile Range		1.5000	
		Skewness		-1.205	.226
		Kurtosis		1.348	.447
	2 or 3 sessions	Mean		5.686624	.0853804
		95% Confidence Interval for Mean	Lower Bound	5.517973	

		Upper Bound	5.855275	
	5% Trimmed Mean		5.770948	
	Median		6.000000	
	Variance		1.144	
	Std. Deviation		1.0698128	
	Minimum		1.6000	
	Maximum		7.0000	
	Range		5.4000	
	Interquartile Range		1.3500	
	Skewness		-1.141	.194
	Kurtosis		1.566	.385
3+ sessions	Mean		5.911814	.0635331
	95% Confidence Interval for Mean	Lower Bound	5.786650	
		Upper Bound	6.036979	
	5% Trimmed Mean		6.002110	
	Median		6.100000	
	Variance		.957	
	Std. Deviation		.9780795	
	Minimum		1.3000	
	Maximum		7.0000	
	Range		5.7000	
	Interquartile Range		1.3500	
	Skewness		-1.357	.158
	Kurtosis		2.579	.315

www.ingramcontent.com/pod-product-compliance
Lightning Source LLC
Chambersburg PA
CBHW041622220426
43662CB00001B/23